Net-Generation Student Motivation to Attend Community College

Shalom Michael Akili

University Press of America,® Inc.
Lanham • Boulder • New York • Toronto • Plymouth, UK

Copyright © 2015 by University Press of America,® Inc.
4501 Forbes Boulevard, Suite 200, Lanham, Maryland 20706
UPA Aquisitions Department (301) 459-3366

Unit A, Whitacre Mews, 26-34 Stannary Street, London SE11 4AB

Library of Congress Control Number: 2014944035
ISBN: 978-0-7618-6434-9 (cloth : alk. paper)—ISBN: 978-0-7618-6435-6 (electronic)

∞™ The paper used in this publication meets the minimum requirements of American National Standard for Information Sciences Permanence of Paper for Printed Library Materials, ANSI/NISO Z39.48-1992.

I would like to dedicate this project to Dr. Adrienne L. Anderson,
I would not have been able to make it through the journey
or accomplish this achievement without you.
I have learned a lot from your teachings that will not only help me
become more successful, but made me a better person.
Thank you for everything you have done for me and I will never forget.

Contents

Acknowledgments

To all my family and friends who helped me through this process—thank you. I wish to express my deepest appreciation for Dr. Ember Lee, with helping throughout the process in learning about research methodology. Dr. Kate Andrews and Dr. Nickson, the most sincere thanks, thank you for all of your help and dedication with allowing me to finish this project.

Chapter One

Introduction

This study explored the motivation of net-generation students to stay in college. The community college is a system of education that allows students a second chance to be successful in life (Merrow, 2007). In a community college, students are able to attain two years of college education as a path to receiving certificates from career training programs, an associate's degree, or a baccalaureate (Agnes & Guralnik, 2002). As community colleges are second-chance institutions, a student's motivation will lead him or her to make the decision to accept the challenge and attempt to gain an education. Once a student has matriculated into a two-year college, various factors will allow them to persist through college. A part of the problem is student motivation: the student needs to obtain enough motivation to decide whether to accept or decline the second chance and continue until the educational goal is complete. Therefore, this study explored (a) college student persistence with (b) motivation for college (c) and self-efficacy.

It is important for community colleges to understand college students' persistence in order to keep students in college as well as to motivate students for college. Student retention has been an on-going issue for the past decade, and the graduation rates in the

United States continue to be approximately 50% (Swail, 2004). Dey and Hurtado (2010) explained:

> Student retention will remain an important area of institutional accountability, and we can expect more institutions will begin to follow closely the progress of students and make effort to improve their college experiences. Trends in student graduation rates have redefined persistence such that it must be monitored from year to year and over a longer time span. Administrators, legislators, and the general public are becoming increasingly concerned about institutional retention rates, and new federal regulations required that institutions report these rates. (p. 335).

If student retention is a part of institutional accountability, this term needs to be clarified. Retention is based on the university college student and has been defined as completion of a program on-time (within four years), completing a program, or maintaining throughout a year with the completion of a certain number of units (Wild & Ebbers, 2002). Retention pertains to students entering into a community college and completing their degrees at the same college within a two-year period. Persistence pertains to a student who enters into a community college and completes the desired goal. Wild and Ebbers (2002) stated: "One definition of retention applied in community colleges is phrased as a persistence rate, and it may be helpful for purposes of definition in that it begins to consider goals other than graduation rates" (p. 506).

Considering the dynamics of a community college, measuring students staying in college versus leaving college through college student persistence would be more useful than measuring retention. Wild and Ebbers (2002) suggested that a definition for persistence of college students could be the percentage of graduates and students persisting or maintaining through the fall and spring semesters, transferring to a four-year program, completing a certificate, and completing a degree. Additionally, the standard measuring scale to determine retention is from the point of view of a traditional student. This would be ineffective in comparison with non-traditional students (Wild & Ebbers, 2002) because, as Wlodkowski (2008) has noted, "Today, 73 percent of all college students can be identified as nontraditional learners" (p. 32). According to Kalsner (1991), less than 15% of student departures are removals; therefore, 85% (or more) of attrition is voluntary (Wild & Ebbers, 2002). The desired goal of a student in a community college could be to complete an 11-month program, attain 12 units in a particular area in order to gain employment, or take courses for the enjoyment of learning a new craft or skill. Therefore, by definition, retention would not apply, although persistence would apply. Persistence can affect retention, but retention cannot affect persistence, because the difference is based on goal attainment and success. If a student considered that 12 units were sufficient, and that a grade point average of 2.8 was a success, then the they would consider that they had achieved their goal and were successful. What is proposed is that an understanding persistence can motivate and encourage students to pursue higher education further, past the units, certificates, and associate degree. This understanding will allow community colleges to better serve their student population.

Based on definition and statistics, community colleges need to acknowledge and understand student motivation in order to improve college student persistence. Understanding the student's experience can affect learning and the motivation of students in their journey of defining success. Therefore, motivation is critical: "Motivation is recognized as a critical need for a society that is clearly worried about its future" (Maehr & Midgley, 1991, p. 400). The US Department of Education, Assistant Secretary for Educational Research and Improvement explained the importance of understanding motivation:

> That is why this question of teacher, student, and parent motivation is one of the single most important questions we face. Because motivation is a multifaceted issue touching many dimen-

sions of education, we want each center to address it. We also want more scholars—both inside and outside the federal education research system—to explore it (Maehr & Midgley, 1991, p. 400).

Even though motivation has become an important aspect of student persistence, it is still an unknown concept when pertaining to college students. Kuh et.al. (2008) explained, "It is not clear to what extent student engagement and other measures of effective educational practice contribute to achievement and persistence over and above student ability" (p. 452).

The many facets that influence college student persistence are relatively unknown. However, Anderson (2003) has identified that, "The best predictor of student persistence in college is the student's own motivation/desire to persist. Therefore, the best retention services are clarify, focus, and build student motivation and address those issues which diminish student motivation" (p. 1). Anderson (2003) asserted that persistence and dropping out are both decisions that students make. Students being able to be successful at what they consider success will determine the persistence of students. If, as noted above, success is defined by gaining 12 units or completing a certificate program, then students will choose to persist until the goal is attained.

The student chooses to gain an education and chooses to be successful in higher education. Students will explore their own abilities to complete a task and for this reason, self-efficacy needs to be explored. Students who fail will drop out on their own, students are not forced to drop out of college. Therefore, the effects of college can be discouragement, disappointment, and lack of confidence, as opposed to lack of ability and dismissal (Anderson, 2003). Additionally, Wlodkowski (2008) stated, "70 percent of current jobs require some form of post-secondary education" (p. 25). This may be part of the student motivation to continue school. Students must be sufficiently motivated to rely on their ability to complete difficult tasks. Motivations for students may include bettering themselves, to obtain a successful career, and to earn enough to ensure future financial stability.

As noted above, the change in student demographics and the shift to incorporating a more non-traditional student body has created the need to acknowledge this non-traditional group of students. This will influence the net-generation students as to whether to persist in college. This is important because the net-generation, currently, is the majority in the population in the United States (Tapscott, 2009). An exploration such as this requires developing an understanding of the students by looking at their generation because each generation will have a unique set of beliefs, values, and mentality. When exploring student persistence and motivations of past generations, it is important to consider the current generation, because this generation has a different set values and belief systems than previous generations. The values of the previous generation will influence the next generation (Carlson, Deloitte, & Touche, n.d.), which can, in turn, affect the students' motivation to accept or decline the second chance by attending a community college. For example, the veteran generation influenced loyalty with baby boomers within the workforce, whereas generation x originated a different value with loyalty in the workplace that had been influenced by the baby boomers (Karp, Fuller, & Sirias, 2002).

The contemporary generation is referred to in this study as the *net-generation*, although it has many other names, such as generation y, gen y-ers, millennials, digital natives, or the net-generation (Elam, Stratton, & Gibson, 2007; Lowe & Skarl, 2009; Price, 2010; Tapscott, 2009). This generation has developed a new set of values about which there is little research. Understanding the new values and beliefs that the net-generation has for education, community colleges can influence college persistence, motivate student for college, and increase self-efficacy that will allow this generation to be successful in college. Current knowledge about this generation—although sparse—demonstrates that this generation is in college attempting to get an education (Price, 2010). The net generation is not only in college, it is also an intricate part of society, and their influence has power with the next generation. Therefore, it is essential to understand and explore ways to influence persistence, motivation, and self-efficacy of the net generation.

College student persistence is an ongoing and important issue in education. Along with persistence, intrinsic motivation is a factor that will influence a college student in their desire to persist in college. Another factor of college student persistence is student self-efficacy. Future generations will be influenced by college students' persistence; thereby the ramifications of college student persistence are an important concern to society.

THE PURPOSE OF THE STUDY

This research study has developed a conceptual framework that can empower educational institutions to retain students and allow students to persist through education.

RESEARCH QUESTIONS

The research questions identified the social norms of community college students and determined to what extent they influenced the learner and the educational institution. The following research questions directed the study:

1. How do students develop their identity in college?
2. Why did students choose college?
3. How successful are students in college?

LIMITATIONS AND DELIMITATIONS

Limitations

Student availability was a significant limitation to this study, given the effects of the school budget and class availability. State funding was identified as an issue that impacted availability of first-year students, with budget cuts there may not be classes available for students to matriculate into college. Student honesty, which is a critical element in gaining information in the interviewing process, was also a limitation to this study. Time constraints were another limitation, based on my need to complete the study before the second school year began and students become too busy to participate.

Delimitations

Focusing on the net-generation of students and their motivation was a delimiting process. The location for the proposed study, San Diego, California, also provided delimitation. Although San Diego has a diverse population, the city does not reflect every person in the world, thereby sampling one community college in San Diego reflected only a sample of the population. For future studies, focus groups could be conducted at other educational systems, such as K–12, university or four-year institutions, and private institutions could provide knowledge pertaining to the community college system, however, the gathering of data for this proposed study will not include these systems. From each educational system, the community college is the most diverse which the reason for this delimitation.

DEFINITION OF TERMS

The following definitions provide a context and meaning for this proposed study.

Net-Generation

Agnes & Guralnik (2002) defined generations as the average of thirty years between the births of people. Generation describes the group of people who have the same experience, attitudes, and share a commonality (Agnes & Guralnik, 2002). The cutoff dates for each generation depend on the interpretation of the scholar or author. However, each different interpretation leaves an age gap between generations (Lowe & Skarl, 2009). For this study people born between 1980 and 2000 were considered to be of the net-generation.

College Student Persistence

Persistence can be defined as a desire and behavior of a student to stay in college from the first year until the completion of the degree (Troxel, 2010). There are numerous factors and influences with persistence and retention that affect students' persistence in college. Persistence pertains to a student who enters into a community college and completes the desired goal. Wild and Ebbers (2002) suggested that, "One definition of retention applied in community colleges is phrased as a persistence rate, and it may be helpful for purposes of definition in that it begins to consider goals other than graduation rates" (p. 506).

Motivation

Brophy (2010) defined motivation as "a theoretical construct used to explain initiation direction, intensity, persistence, and quality of behavior, especially goal-direct" (p. 3). Wlokoski (2010) stated, "Motivation binds emotion to action. It creates as well as guides purposeful behavior" (p. 2). Motivation explains the reason why people perform certain behaviors and think in their current thought processes (Wlodkowski, 2008). Moreover, Wlodkowski (2008) mentioned "motivation as purposeful" (p. 3).

Self-Efficacy

Bandura (1997) indicated that, "Perceived self-efficacy is a judgment of one's ability to organize and execute given types of performances, whereas an outcome expectation is a judgment of the likely consequence such performances will produce" (p. 21). Self-efficacy includes students' beliefs about their capability to perform at a particular level in certain tasks or events in their lives. According to Bandura (1997), "Raising the belief in their efficacy makes them more perseverant" (p. 216). For a student in a community college, confidence in their ability to be successful is paramount to ensure success.

IMPORTANCE OF THE STUDY

The importance of this study is the resulting conceptual framework, which can empower junior colleges to retain and motivate students to persist through higher education. This study has added to the body of knowledge of higher education by giving faculty, staff, and administrators an understanding of how students feel about their education and their learning experience. This study also provides an understanding of the factors that influence students when they are attempting to achieve their goal of obtaining an education and of their motivation for continuing their education. However, there was minimal empirical data in the literature that explored student motivation and education from a general perspective. This study therefore explored college student persistence, along with intrinsic motivation, to reveal how college students persist (as it relates to the net-generation) and provided insight to the factors that influence the net-generation of students to persist through college.

Chapter Two

Review of Literature

INTRODUCTION

The literature review is an exploration of the community college system as it relates to factors of persistence and the characteristics of net-generation students. The community college system's programs, purpose, and history make it a unique educational institution in the United States (Pusser & Levin, 2009). Community colleges serve the broadest demographic student population of any educational system (Pulliam & Patten, 1999). Persistence in the community college setting relates to completion of individual students' intended goals (post-secondary certification or degree completion). This review focused on the multiple factors of persistence that result in success or incompletion (Williams, 2010).

The particular students that were the focus of this proposed study were all from the net-generation (Tapscott, 2010). As this demographic comprises the largest sector of the college age population, their influence is significant (Elam et al., 2007; Elmore, 2010; Howe & Straus, 2000; Lowe & Skari, 2009; Rainer & Rainer, 2011; Tapscott, 2010). Net-generation members have characteristics that are unique to the overall population (Elam et al., 2007; Elmore, 2010; Howe & Straus, 2000; Lowe & Skari, 2009; Rainer

& Rainer, 2011; Tapscott, 2010). This study explored those characteristics in depth as they relate to the factors of college persistence.

COMMUNITY COLLEGE SYSTEM
IN THE UNITED STATES

The community college is an institution in which high school graduates can enter college or returning college students can go back to
school and earn an associate's degree, earn credits to transfer to a
four-year university, or students can gain a certificate through a
vocational program (Pusser & Levin, 2009). The community college is a unique higher educational institution because of the variety of programs available for students and the services it provides to
society (Pusser & Levin, 2009). Students have another opportunity
at achieving a baccalaureate degree by attending community colleges. Additionally, returning students can gain specific skills
through vocational programs and earn a certificate that will make
the student eligible for employment. According to a statistical re-
port from the American Association of Community Colleges
(AACC, 2012), programs that are offered at community colleges
include personal and culinary services, liberal arts, precision and
production, engineering, and military services, just to name a few.
For example, students desiring to work in a beauty salon can earn a
certificate or an associate degree in cosmetology to gain employment, or a student who desires to become an auto mechanic can
earn a degree or certificate in engineering that will make the student eligible for employment. Pusser and Levin (2009) explained
that approximately 10% of students in community colleges already
have their baccalaureate degrees, and enrolled into the community
college to either learn a skill in a different field or to pursue a
passion to learn another language. Therefore, community colleges
seem to promote lifelong learning as well as providing a degree or
certificate.

History of Community Colleges

Historically, the first junior or community colleges did not open until the 1870s, but it was not until the early 1900s that community colleges began to grow, with more than 600 operational community colleges emerging over that decade (Cohen & Kisker, 2010). Pulliam and Patten (1999) pointed out, "By 1997, more than 1,473 junior colleges and community colleges were operating with a combined enrollment of 5 million students" (p. 160). In 2006, more than six million students enrolled in college (Pulliam & Patten, 1999).

The junior college or community college system was considered to be a successful innovation, defined as "institutions offering two years of instruction" (Cohen & Kisker, 2010, p. 120). The leaders of this innovation suggested that they would not be true leaders of research if the freshman and sophomores classes were not retained (Cohen & Kisker, 2010). The inspirational force to further higher education was the increasing number of high school graduates (Cohen & Kisker, 2010). Community colleges were intended to retain the freshman and sophomore classes at the university level by providing a two-year education for transfer to other educational institutions (Pulliam & Patten, 1999), aid in the increasing high school graduation rates (Cohen & Kisker, 2010), and open the door for a diverse population of students (Pulliam & Patten, 1999). A rush toward education occurred (Pulliam & Patten, 1999). Through assisting universities and high schools, by either promoting higher education or retaining students, community colleges are furthering society's education (Cohen & Kisker, 2010). The community college is a pathway to both the baccalaureate degree as well as to successful careers that will guarantee their importance in the nation's educational system (Cohen & Kisker, 2010). Currie and Newson (cited in Cohen & Kisker, 2010) explained that this encouraged students to view education as a means of increasing income, although the risk is accepting high tuition as an investment for their future to be financially secure.

Approximately 39% of the college student population is enrolled in community colleges (Pusser & Levin, 2009), with an additional 3.6 million (approximately) students engaged in continuing education and noncredit courses annually (Pusser & Levin, 2009). The age range of this increasing student population is primarily 18–29 and the average age of a student in community college is 29 years of age (AACC, 2012; Phillippe & Patton, 2000). In terms of ethnicity, (Kahlenberg, 2010) identified that he student population was at first primarily white, comprising 73% of community college students in 1994. However, this decreased to 58% in 2006, while the minority non-white increased population from 1994 to 2006 to 33%, reflecting a change in the diversity of the student population in community colleges. Currently, of students enrolled in college, 53.8% work part-time and 83.6% work full-time, meaning that 30% of students balance working full-time with maintaining full-time student status, which is 12 units or more (Burgess, 2012). Lastly, community colleges used to receive enough funding for student grants, but college and governmental spending has strayed away from grants and is now moving toward student loans (33.5% of Pell grants go to community colleges), which means debt for students (AACC, 2012). Consequently, this affected student's eligibility for financial aid because students are unable to receive financial aid if the aid is not available or difficult to obtain. Additionally, the AACC (2012) stated that the majority of the jobs by the year 2014 will require some type of higher education.

STUDENT DEVELOPMENT THEORY

Student development theory emerged in response to the increasing numbers and diversity of the student population in colleges as well as the need to provide the best learning experience for students.

Student development theory evolved through the fields of psychology and sociology to convey to educators the relationship to students' learning capabilities (Evans, Forney, Guido, Patton, & Renn, 2010). Evans, Forney, Guido, Patton, & Renn (2010) noted that Frank Parsons "was the first to articulate a match between personal characteristics and particular occupations to determine the best fit for individuals in the work environment" (p. 8).

Furthermore, historical events changed the demographics of the student population and the manner in which students were educated. Examples included shifts in societal needs in the United States that required people to develop new and different skills to gain employment (McClellan, Stringer, & Associates, 2009). McClellan et al. stated:

> The Service Readjustment Act in 1944 (as known as the G.I. Bill) spurred huge increase in college enrollments across the United States. The students who came to campus were different in many important ways from those who had come before them. (p. 9)

Student demographics changed when the students who were unable to matriculate into college before had the opportunity to do so. This student population that began to matriculate into college consisted of African Americans, Latinos, Native Americans, and women (Cohen & Kisker, 2010). This would be the introduction of diversity in higher education. These events diversified the demographics of the student population in higher education.

PSYCHOSOCIAL THEORY

Students in college are attempting to achieve a goal, and therefore they find that in college it is necessary to complete small tasks in order to obtain the larger goal. During the process of obtaining the goal or completion of a task, students experience a developmental phase. Psychosocial theory is appropriate to help understand students during the developmental phase. Psychosocial theory was intended to explain a particular development with tasks or stages in life with humans; some of the tasks or stages include thinking, emotions, behaviors, values, beliefs, interpersonal relationships, and the relationship with oneself (Chickering & Reisser, 1993). Human emotions, thinking, and the development of emotions and thinking created an interest "in how people thought about themselves and the world but also in how they felt, behaved, and interpreted the meaning of experience" (Chickering & Reisser, 1993, p. 21). Psychosocial theory can be used to explain the development of motivation: when an individual desires to learn who he or she is as a person and has a sense of identity, then the individual will understand the personal motivation for the tasks he or she desires to perform.

STUDENT PERSISTENCE IN THE COMMUNITY COLLEGE

To understand community college students, it is important to understand why students persist through college. Persistence is defined as a desire and behavior of a student to stay in college from the first year until the completion of the degree, and the words retention and persistence have been used interchangeably within higher education (Troxel, 2010). This study focused primarily on persistence. Numerous factors and influences affect student's persistence in college. This review of literature explored the factors of (a) intrinsic motivation, (b) self-efficacy, (c) interpersonal relationships, and (d) financial issues that affect student persistence in college.

IDENTITY DEVELOPMENT

Motivation is a factor that can determine college student persistence. Nevitt Sanford (cited in Chickering & Reisser, 1993) advanced Erickson's theory by describing the changing designs in which college students think, feel, and behave. Chickering's identity development theory borrowed from the previous work of Erikson, Keagan, and Loevinger (Chickering & Reisser, 1993). As a part of psychosocial theory, Chickering's seven vectors theory was used to examine student identity. According to McClellan et al., (2009), Chickering's seven vectors explained the development of students as how students learn, grow, and develop. The seven vectors signify, change with severity and direction, path of developing competence, regulating emotions, having an identity, obtaining autonomy, having integrity, and developing relationships (McClellan et al., 2009). Of course, each student is different, so each student will transition through each point of his or her life at different times, sectors, and instances (Chickering & Reisser, 1993). This is the reason that it is important to look into the transitional period of students: to determine where the student is in the growth process and whether the student is at a certain level in the growth process that will provide the motivation to attempt higher education, continue, or finish.

Intrinsic Motivation

Different things will motivate students in their growth processes at different times. Brophy (2010) defined motivation as "a theoretical construct used to explain initiation direction, intensity, persistence, and quality of behavior, especially goal-direct" (p. 3). Kit-Ling (2009) identified two types of motivation: intrinsic and extrinsic. Intrinsic motivation was viewed as the personal belief or values that reflect behaviors, characteristics, and emotional aspects of students that is motivational (Kit-Ling, 2009). To explain intrinsic motivation, Brophy (2010) used the example of a prisoner sentenced to life. Even though the prisoner will never get out of jail, the prisoner can focus on his or her life values and beliefs by gaining an education in the prison system, reading books, engaging in physical exercise, and being at peace within oneself. Contrarily, the prisoner can have alternative values and beliefs and become depressed, angry, and blame others for his or her misfortunes.

Extrinsic Motivation

Extrinsic motivation is some type of reward for motivation: it is something given to the person for motivation (Kit-Ling, 2009). Extrinsic motivation using the prisoner example would be getting out of prison, either waiting on a document that can lead to getting out of prison, a person with a testimony that can change the outcome of the verdict, or the next meeting with an attorney. Developing an understanding of the cyclical nature of human development and not disregarding extrinsic motivation by solely accepting the intrinsic motivation is useful: it reveals that there are two parts to motivation and both parts have an effect on each other. Extrinsic motivation is important because there are objects or external things that can internally motivate people. For example, if a student completes a degree program and the reward is a new car, the student will intrinsically motivate him/herself by incorporating proper study habits, surrounding him/herself with successful students, and showing signs of determination. This is to show that extrinsic motivation is important, but it is also important to find a balance between the two and understand the significance of the roles of both intrinsic and extrinsic motivation. For this review of literature, the primary focus was on intrinsic motivation, while recognizing the role of external motivation.

Development is cyclical because it can occur in multiple instances; for example, age is not a factor, it depends on individuals' growth and where they are in their growing process (Chickering & Reisser, 1993). During the growth process, multiple factors (such as the environmental, social interactions, interpersonal growth and understanding autonomy, are the elements an individual will encounter during the journey of self-discovery (Chickering & Reisser,

1993). Development is cyclical because the development is inter-changeable and can potentially have two factors occurring at the same time (Chickering & Reisser, 1993). Understanding the developmental process allow for will further understanding of a student's identity. Students are continuously balancing their own development and success within the community colleges, whether it is positive or negative, and the relationship affects their intrinsic motivation to persist through college (Evans et al., 2010). An understanding of the intrinsic motivation of students enhances understanding of what matriculates students into college and allows students to persist.

CHOICE THEORY

As community colleges became popular and an intricate part of society, students gained the choice of whether to accept or decline higher education. According to Edwards (2009), choice theory hypothesized that human behavior involved emotions and thinking. People have control of their behavior and thinking, albeit a limited ability to choose and regulate their emotions and behavior. Choice theory is used to explain that people are motivated by five basic needs, which are (a) survival, (b) love and belonging, (c) power, (d) freedom, and (e) fun, and to examine how people attempt to fulfill these needs (Edwards, 2009; Loyd, 2005; Mottern, 2008). Loyd (2005) noted that, "There exists an interconnection between needs satisfaction and behavior" (p. 5). Choice theory resembles Maslow's hierarchy of needs, although scholars have identified the differences between of each theory: Maslow's theory puts needs in sequence, where one is not achieved without the other, whereas Glasser's theory is cyclical and a person can have more than one need occurring at the same time (Edwards, 2009). Additionally, choice theory describes learning as a lifelong, continuous process, regardless of what age the individual may be. As Mottern (2008) explained:

> Choices begin to be made in infancy and continue through the physiological developmental stages of childhood, adolescence, young, middle and older adulthood. As individuals age, they may or may not become consciously aware of their Basic Needs. Individuals may or may not develop strategies to satisfy their Basic Needs. All individuals will, however, progress from relying on others to satisfy their Needs to making conscious choices about their behaviors that satisfy their own Basic Needs. This progression, from others satisfying Needs to self-satisfying Needs is development. Development is not sequential but is progressive. Individuals do not pass through various stages of development but do become progressively better at making choices to meet their Needs. This progression is noted by a lessening of motivation to fulfill the Need. (p. 35).

As individuals begin to understand the process of their own growth and how this relates to the basic needs in life, individuals are motivated for certain needs, and motivation for other needs declines. An example is social acceptance. Individuals tend to be motivated to be accepted in certain social surroundings and the transition from having high motivation for social acceptance to a low motivation for social acceptance may or may not happen, contingent on the individual's growth process and understanding of his/her basic needs.

Choice theory began with treating adolescent girls with behavioral problems. However, even though this is the origin of the treatment, Glasser believed that "people are responsible for the choices they make in life" (cited in Edwards, 2009, p. 263). Glasser's theory suggested that people experience the world and create the world around them in order to fulfill their basic needs, and those who are unable to fulfill their basic needs become depressed, self-destructive, or unmotivated (cited in Loyd, 2005). Research has shown that if high school students' needs are not met, it contributes to destructive behavior such as low motivation for academics and performance, and unproductive social relationships (Loyd, 2005). Even though this has been shown in high school students, the same behavior is, arguably, likely to be shown after graduation from high school and entering into the community college. Choice theory sets a foundation to understand the learner, it is understood that all behaviors have a purpose, thereby understanding the behavior leads to regulating behavior (Blance, 2004).

Glasser's choice theory is appropriate for discovering the reason students choose to matriculate into college and persist through college. Choice theory may help to answer the questions why students choose college and what thoughts, feelings, and behaviors motivate students to choose college. This model suggested that people's motivation is based on five basic needs, what are the five basic needs of students. Survival, seeking love and belonging, freedom, and fun in college are basic needs that college student can potentially have. With this continuous lifelong process of fulfilling basic needs— whether this is one at a time or fulfilling multiple needs at the same time—satisfying the basic needs is a lifetime of understanding and contingent upon where a person is in their life, the basic needs will change.

Relationships

The fact that it is not mandatory for students to matriculate into college gives students a choice to either choose or not choose college. Additionally, while in college students will choose to have a relationship with their college by attending events on campus, becoming involved in clubs, athletics, or student government, and communicating with faculty. Ultimately, students choose the type of relationship that they have with college, but colleges play a role by providing students with the best learning environment (Lau, 2003). Jensen (2011) suggested that student socioeconomic status affects student choice and cultural capital. Swail (2004) indicated that students are not psychologically prepared for higher education.

This is difficult for community colleges, because of the demand that the student body can have on community colleges (Wild & Ebbers, 2002). Swail (2004) claimed that upper echelon higher educational institutions influence student persistence because when a student is not succeeding, the institution brings the student closer by introducing the student to different resources available to help the student. However, the availability of funding for these types of services is not available to every higher educational institution (Educational Policy Institute, 2002). Fortunately, the relationship that a student has with the college can influence the collegiate experience and influence student outcomes if the services are provided (Strauss & Volkwein, 2004).

The motivation to have a relationship with a professor or teacher at a college can affect college student persistence. Currently, there is a disconnection with students and teachers, as well as with students and the school. Glasser (1998) has suggested that if enough discipline is applied in the classroom, then the students will learn, although choice theory indicates that if the discipline conflicts with a student's needs in the classroom then the student will potentially not learn because it does not fit their needs. The analogy used by Glasser (1998) was based on the saying that *you can lead a horse to water but cannot make it drink*, if a student is forced into doing something he/she does not wish to do, the student will rebel or become disruptive to the classroom. Instead, students who do not have a strong supportive social network are more at risk of not being able to recognize and understand their own basic needs, this results in deviant behaviors such as not attending class, failing classes from not completing assignments, or social isolation because students are not able to meet their needs. Loyd (2005) showed that in some cases, students are not knowledgeable of how to meet their own basic needs.

Blance (2004) explained the importance of relationships, and that students who have positive and quality relationships are more engaged in the classroom, which can lead to being successful in the class as well as in college. The idea that a good teacher can motivate any student and a bad teacher demotivates students is a false assumption: if a student is adamant about not learning, regardless of the dexterity of the teacher, the student will not learn (Glasser, 1998). Additionally, Glasser (1998) contested the traditional ideologies of education because it does not correlate with the students' needs, especially depending on where the student is in his or her growing process. The connection is that in community colleges, the students may not have an understanding of their own behavior nor have control over their own behavior, and with this lack of understanding, students may not know what it is they want to do in life.

The relationships that students have with each other will influence their motivation and persistence. Edwards (2009) pointed out that, "Glasser asserts that lack of connectedness to a valued social network is the primary source of many human problems, such as social-emotional distress, drug addiction, violence, crime, and school failure" (p. 263). Brophy (2010) explained that students who alienate themselves usually are not successful in college. In addition, in colleges that promote diversity, students are more likely to be engaged, involved, and successful (Brophy, 2010; Swail, 2004).

Understanding an individual's basic needs is a continuous process and wherever an individual is in their development process will determine the student's needs. For example, the social environment can be a potential factor with the individual's needs. A student in college may or may not be motivated to attend class because the need to be social with friends is a more important need. The social environment factor is important in education because teachers and colleges would need to understand the students as far as where they are in their life process and what needs they are motivated to fulfill. If the student understands their needs at the point in the life process that they are in currently, the approach to motivate the student is to keep them engaged in the classroom according to their stated needs.

Financial Issues

King (2003) stated that students' choices in college at certain times are financial and will affect whether the student decides to be persistent in college. With high tuition costs, students' lifestyles are affected by having to make financial decisions (King, 2003). Furthermore, the students' backgrounds will affect the financial decision to choose college and persist. For example, some important financial considerations are family size (whether the parent/s can support all their children through college), students working either full-time or part-time, the students' work schedule conflicting with class schedule, family income, available grants, scholarships, and financial aid. Leppel (2005) stated that a student's values and beliefs about having a successful financial future will determine their persistence in college. When a student has future-oriented thinking about obtaining a high paying job, paying high tuition and accepting the financial demands are viewed as an investment in the student's future (Leppel, 2005). Thus, patience and financial success are important factors to consider if a student is going to persist in college (Leppel, 2005).

THEORY OF SELF-EFFICACY

According to Leppel (2005), persistence is evident in the example of a student who enters into an educational institution and completes the degree or program, or a student who enters an educational institution to complete a degree or program, but transfers to another educational institution to complete the degree or program. Bandura's (1997) self-efficacy theory was used to explore some of the reasons why students continue to stay in college to complete their education. According to Bandura's (1997) theory of self-efficacy, "Perceived self-efficacy is a judgment of one's ability to organize and execute given types of performances, whereas an outcome expectation is a judgment of the likely consequence such performances will produce" (p. 21). King (2003) stated that every day students make the decision to persist, based on their abilities. The abilities could be based on success either in a program or in a class, contingent upon what the student has defined as success. Additionally, community colleges would benefit from having more information about the choices that students make and the ramification of their choices, this will give community colleges insight on intervention programs that can help or influence students to increase their levels of persistence (King, 2003). College student persistence is also a part of the social interaction that can influence thought processes, behaviors, and persistence. Extrinsic influences can affect emotions and the intrinsic environment. The physical nature of the stimulus can have an effect on the behavior of the individual and can place potential constraints on their abilities.

Bandura's (1997) theory of self-efficacy served to examine students' beliefs about their capability to perform at a particular level in certain tasks in their lives: "Raising the belief in their efficacy makes them more perseverant" (Bandura, 1997, p. 216). Self-efficacy looks at the students intrinsically to see how they view themselves.

Leppel (2005) stated that, "The student's assessment of the benefits and costs of a college education depends on the background traits of that individual. These traits include demographic characteristics and socioeconomic status, skills, abilities, and aptitudes, and initial attitudes and intentions" (p. 226). When students are looking at themselves, their decisions are based on their own understanding of how well they will perform and at what level. Bandura (1997) explained the potential consequences of career choice and efficacy:

Career decision making is not simply a matter of picking a particular occupational pursuit but rather of developing facility in solving problems when things are not easily predictable. Nor is it simply a matter of learning problem-solving skills. People who lack confidence in their judgment have difficulty making decisions and sticking with them even if they have been taught the strategies for doing so (p. 427).

A student who has already chosen an area of study is confident in his/her ability to complete the job, meaning that he/she is successful at the position. On the other hand, a student can be confident of his/her ability in a particular career and pursue the career by going to college, but during the process of obtaining the degree to match the career, the student may re-evaluate pursuing the degree based on his/her success in the degree program. If, for example, the student is not performing well in the program, the student will begin to reflect on whether the career choice is a good fit. This process of evaluation is based on self-perception and success.

Another factor is students' past-experience with certain tasks. The success of the task is contingent upon the influence of the student's behavior, attitude, and intentions for future and current tasks (Leppel, 2005). For example, if a student in elementary school was not been successful in math classes, he or she may be apprehensive about taking math classes in college based on past-experience. Jensen (2011) found that grade point average is one of the most significant predictors of student persistence. The success of students in their past-experiences will determine their persistence in college. In the metaphor of a teeter-totter, self-efficacy can go in either direction, it can elevate a student to motivate them to work harder, increase intensity, and re-strategize to be successful. Contrarily, it can demotivate students by limiting confidence, limiting engagement, and devaluing the students' feelings toward self.

Determining how students view themselves in the world of academics gives insight on the level of persistence of the individual student. Students may need to have a high success rate with performance to continue and others may use any type of success to fuel their motivation. If a person continues to fail, typically that person will not continue to engage at what they are failing. In the classroom, if a student continues to be unsuccessful, then the student may question, limit, and doubt his/her ability to be successful. On the other hand, if students are successful, then the likelihood of them continuing, putting forth effort, and planning for success will be greater. Williams (2010) stated, "The issues that influence the retention rates of rural students are academic, emotional, social, and financial reasons, or a combination" (p. 365). Even though this example only mentions rural students, the same influence is likely other students in regards to persistence.

NET-GENERATION

The generation with which students identify affects intrinsic motivation and college student persistence. The classification for the present generation has a five-year gap either at the beginning of the year classification or the end (Elam et al., 2007; Lowe & Skari, 2009; Price, 2010; Tapscott, 2010). As noted above, the net generation is classified for this study as those born between 1980 and 2000.

This generation is unique because of the close relationships they have with their parents, which has been looked at as either positive or negative. Some researchers suggest that parents hinder students from learning survival skills, while others consider the close relationships a positive relationship because students learn from their parents (Elam et al., 2007; Lowe & Skari, 2009; Price, 2010; Tapscott, 2010). This close relationship with parents and children is believed to create a sense of entitlement with this generation. Thereby, students of this generation believe that they deserve to gain certain positions or have certain things, even though other generations believe they do not (Elam et al., 2007; Lowe & Skari, 2009; Price, 2010; Tapscott, 2010).

A characteristic of this generation is the high value they place on relationships (Elam et al., 2007; Lowe & Skari, 2009; Price, 2010; Tapscott, 2010). Regardless of what a person can provide, this generation does not interact with an individual if the relationship does not have a positive status (Elam et al., 2007; Lowe & Skari, 2009; Price, 2010; Tapscott, 2010). Therefore, it would be difficult to teach a net-generation student in the classroom if the relationship between the teacher and student is not in good standing. It is important for faculty and community colleges to understand the net generation because the relationship will reflect a generalization of the student's values and belief systems. The information provided about this generation, although sparse, demonstrates they are attempting to get an education and place a high value on education (Price, 2010). The net generation is in college, they are an intricate part of society, and their influence has power with the next generation.

The net-generation characteristics have an impact on the factors of intrinsic motivation, choice, and self-efficacy that determine college student persistence. The parental involvement with net-generation students can influence intrinsic motivation because it will influence the student's identity and how they view themselves (Price, 2010). Students may develop their own identity that will allow them to have beliefs, characteristics, and values that will allow the net-generation student to be successful in college. The net-generation student with the characteristic of entitlement may choose not to matriculate or be persistent in college because of the belief that he/she deserves a degree, certificate, or grade. For example, a net-generation student may have learned all the information in a college course, but may not complete the work to pass the class, although feel they deserve a good grade. The relationships that net-generation students have are given high value; therefore, a net-generation student may not learn as much in a college classroom if they do not like the teacher or have a good relationship with the teacher (Price, 2010).

CONCLUSION TO CHAPTER TWO

College students' intrinsic motivation and persistence are key areas for the net generation. It is important for colleges to understand college student persistence, in order for them to keep students in college and assist students with achieving their goals. Exploring self-efficacy will give colleges the ability to influence students in terms of their ability to complete tasks. This outcome empowers the student to strive to be the best they can be and to increase their tenacity in other tasks as well. Understanding the relationship of this intersection will reveal ways to motivate students to choose college and empower students to persist through college.

Chapter Three

Methodology

Chapter one of this dissertation contained an exploration of the connection of intrinsic motivation, education, and college student persistence. This study explored college students who completed their first year of study to continue to strive for an education in community college. This chapter contains the study design, methods, population and sample, as well as respondent confidentiality that were used to explore the various factors and themes that influence intrinsic motivation and persistence of college students.

RESEARCH DESIGN

A mixed methods approach was used to obtain understanding about intrinsic motivation and persistence of students to gain an education. Creswell (2009) clarified that the mixed methods approach is a combination of qualitative and quantitative research methods. Qualitative methods deal with words: meaning data is collected through interviews, usually consisting of open-ended questions, while the researcher explores the research topic (Creswell, 2009). Creswell (2009) explained that quantitative research deals with numbers; thereby data collection by acquiring numbers through surveys or closed-end questions. A mixed methods approach combines both qualitative and quantitative approaches (Creswell, 2009). This method allows a researcher to gain multiple perspectives about the research topic, thereby not limiting the study. Using the mixed method approach will allow the researcher "to broaden understanding by incorporating both qualitative and quantitative research, or to use one approach to better understand, explain, or build on the results from the other approach" (Creswell, 2009, pp. 204–205). The mixed methods approach therefore provided a better understanding of student motivation and the decision to stay in college. The qualitative aspect of the proposed study served to explore the students' stories and gain information from their experience. The information gained the student stories helped to explain what intrinsically motivates the net-generation college student and the important factors that affect college student persistence. Quantitatively validating the students' stories and testing the student's theories about their stories strengthened the findings of the study. Both quantitative and qualitative data were used in this study to confirm or validate the intrinsic motivation and other factors affecting college student persistence within the sampled participants to gain a better understanding of the larger population. Creswell (2009) explained that the mixed methods approach as: "The use of both approaches in tandem so that the overall strength of a study is greater than either qualitative or quantitative research" (p. 4).

RESEARCH METHODS

The study was framed by three research questions, which were adopted to gain knowledge of the processes of student persistence:

1. How do students develop their identity in college?
2. Why did students choose college?
3. How successful are students in college?

This study implemented the focus group model of Krueger and Casey (2000) to guide data collection and transcription into a contextual text analysis from the information provided by the students participating in the focus group. Transferring the exact language used during the focus group into the text analysis program contributed to the quantitative segment of the study. Students shared past experiences and reflected on themselves with others by exchanging dialogue.

During dialogue, I endeavored to listen to the students with little to no bias. My role as researcher was to listen and learn from the students' explanation of what motivates them to persist in education. A transcriber was be used to further the confidentiality of the participants and to record the responses of the participants to limit bias. After the data from the focus group was collected and analyzed, a survey based on the themes from the focus group was created. The data was quantified to create a web-based survey, and a separate group of students participated for the quantitative segment of the study. The survey used a Likert scale format to allow data collection. Data from the survey was kept confidential by assigning fictitious names to each participant. The data from the web-based survey will be correlated with the data from the focus group students. Once the survey was completed, the participants' role with the quantitative portion of the proposed study was considered to have ended. The data was gathered from the focus group and the survey to conduct a comparative analysis.

POPULATION AND SAMPLING PROCEDURES

The population consisted of students who had completed their first year of community college in Southern California. The age range of students was between 18–25 years of age. This population involved a focus group of 6–10 participants, which was the recommended sample size (Krueger & Casey, 2000; Patton, 2002). Students of various backgrounds, areas of study, and gender were welcomed to participate in the study. The sample consisted of students from San Diego City College in downtown San Diego.

Stratification is important for this population because of the diversity at the community college. Creswell (2009) described stratification as follows: "When randomly selecting people from a population, these characteristics may or may not be present in the sample in the same proportions as the population; stratification ensures their representation. Also identify the characteristics used in stratifying the population" (p. 148). Stratification occurred in this research due to by the students being high school graduates, ranging in age from 18–25, and in the process of obtaining an associate's degree. The associate's degree requirement means that the student has completed four general education courses, three courses within a major or specific area of study, and an additional six courses, not including prerequisites. Students must complete at least 12 units or four courses, regardless of time to complete, because this is the equivalent of a full-time student in a community college.

Each student's accumulative grade point average was identified as either: 4.0, 3.0, 2.0, or 1.0. Students were required to have a grade point average of at least 2.0 for this proposed study, because this is the minimum criterion for participating in community colleges. Lastly, each student participant's working status was identified as either: full-time (40 hours or more per week), part-time (less than 40 and above 20 hours per week), or not working (0 hours per week). This study was multi-cultural, in order to acknowledge different perceptions and experiences and to not exclude anyone (Patton, 2002). Therefore, the study sample was not limited by students' nationality or race and ethnicity was identified. In addition, students of different gender identifications were included (whether they were male, female, transgender, homosexual, or bisexual), so that the experiences of, and information provided by, this group would reveal different perceptions.

Access to the population should be "on location—at the place where the participants come for recreation, shopping, or other purposes" (Krueger and Casey, 2000, p. 76). In this study, the location to place in the venue where participants came to learn and gain an education: San Diego City College. Considering the social dynamics of community colleges and the massive number (2,206,413) of full-year students that attend (AACC, 2012), this was an optimal environment to obtain the stratified sample for the proposed study.

After receiving e-mails and phone calls from the students who interested in participating, one pool of participants was used for the first phase of the study. Another pool was used for the second phase of the study. Once a pool of applicants was obtained, I contacted the chosen participants to organize a day, time, and location for the focus group. This was based on the assertion made by Krueger and Casey (2000) and Patton (2002) that focus groups need to be properly planned. The location of the focus group was an on-campus conference room at San Diego City College, because as a faculty member at the institution, I had access to these facilities. Additionally, an on-campus location for the focus groups helped to protect participants and to ensure confidentiality: a locked classroom on campus provided a very secure location. I conducted the focus groups during times of low activity on the campus to allow for an intimate, comfortable environment.

San Diego City College had the contact information of all the students at the college and aided in the process, so that protection of participants identity was enforced. The sample of the study was from the focus groups; the population consisted of first-year students and students who had completed their first year. San Diego Community College sent e-mails to this population informing students about the second part of the study. For the second portion of the study, the e-mails sent by the college offered a link to the web-based survey, allowing student access. The consent forms were e-mailed to all students who attended the college via e-mail through

San Diego City College. Students were able to contact me directly from the e-mail sent by the college. For part one, the students contacted me for the focus groups; for part two the students who were interested in participating gained access to the web-based survey via the internet.

Part One: Focus Groups

The first part of the study consisted of focus groups, and the interview process was semi-structured using open-ended interview questions. I sometimes asked additional questions, although only for clarification purposes of the participants' responses. Kitzinger (1995) discovered that "focus groups reach the parts that other methods cannot reach, revealing dimensions of understanding that talking with other people who have similar experiences" (pp. 299–300). This suggests that the researcher can gain more out of a focus group, because through dialogue the participants may find commonality with their experiences. For this study, the focus group allowed students to depict their values and beliefs towards deciding to stay in college. As Kitzinger (1995) stated:

> This means that instead of the researcher asking each person to respond to a question in turn, people are encouraged to talk to one another: asking questions, exchanging anecdotes and commenting on each other's experiences and points of view. The method is particularly useful for exploring people's knowledge and experiences and can be used to examine not only what people think but how they think and why they think that way (p. 299).

Students participating in the focus group were San Diego City College students, but they did not know each other; this was a deliberate decision, as people are more likely to share personal information with strangers than people with whom they are already acquainted (Krueger & Casey, 2000). Conducting open-ended questions in the focus group allowed students to familiarize them-selves with each other. The nonthreatening and nonjudgmental en-vironment allowed students to feel comfortable about sharing per-sonal feelings and information, which also increased the level of honesty. As Krueger and Casey (2000) stated, "A focus group is a carefully planned series of discussions designed to obtain percep-tions on a defined area of interest in a permissive, nonthreatening environment" (p. 5). Additionally, Patton (2002) explained, "a se-ries of focus groups will be conducted to get a variety of perspec-tives and increase confidence in whatever patterns emerge" (p. 385). Furthermore, Krueger and Casey (2000) stated:

> Focus groups have proven helpful mostly because they provide an interactive environment. Focus groups enable people to pon-der, reflect, and listen to experiences and opinions of others. This interaction helps participants compare their own personal reality to that of others (p. 16–17).

Through dialogue, students will begin to explain and understand their motivation, why they chose college, and why they continue to stay.

During the focus groups, an audio recording was made. The reason for this was to limit researcher bias and to extract the infor-mation from the dialogue into *Diction 6.0* software. A transcriber was present during the focus groups. *Microsoft Word and Microsoft Excel* software were used to save the responses of the focus group participants. In addition, the information was stored on a computer, and only I knew the passcode. I stored the focus group session data immediately after the focus group session concluded.

During the focus group session, I repeated what each participant said for further clarity about each of the students' responses. This allowed the participants to feel that they were being properly heard and represented. For the context text analysis, I used Diction 6.0 software. The program was installed on one computer that was password-protected and only I knew the password. The themes that emerge from the focus group will be used to create and develop questions for the web-based survey.

During the focus groups, the students began to understand what motivated them and to recognize that their decisions to attend and stay in college were conscious decisions. The factors that persuaded their decision were considered to be the drivers for student motivation. The students reached this understanding concept through dialogue. Kitzinger (1995) explained: "The idea behind the focus group method is that group processes can help people to explore and clarify their views" (p. 299).

Sample Size

I collaborated with San Diego City College to recruit a stratified sample of 20–40 students to conduct three or four focus groups consisting of 6–10 students each from the San Diego City College student population. Patton (2002) explained: "sampling for focus groups typically involves bringing together people of similar backgrounds and experiences to participate in a group interview about major issues that affect them" (p. 236). The criteria for the students in the sample was that they were currently enrolled, between the ages of 18–25, had at least a 2.0 accumulative GPA, were in pursuit of an associate's degree, and had completed at least 12 units or four college courses.

The fact that the study involved college students made it necessary to confine the study to enrolled college students. The reason for the limited age range (of 18–25) was that students who were older would have been more influenced by the previous generation (generation x or baby boomers, depending on the age of the parents). The oldest age (25) was considered to show a change in the generational values and beliefs systems, and students closer to the age of 18 would definitely show characteristics of the net generation. The Office of Institutional Research and Planning (2012) at

San Diego City College identified that 18–24 year old students comprised 54% of the student population. Of those students who attempted over 12 units, 48% of the students earned the units in fall 2011 (although this is not broken down by age) and student persistence for those between the ages of 18–24 was around 60%. Students who have an accumulative grade point average of 2.0 were considered to show signs of persistence: for example, if a student did not perform well in either classes one semester and received a grade point average below a 2.0 for that semester, but the following semester received a 3.5 grade point average, this result would show persistence and motivation of the student.

Participants were limited to students who were attempting to gain an associate's degree, because community colleges offer a wide variety of programs. Some of the programs in the community colleges span less than a year, which would not show persistence: focusing on associate degree students ensured a population of students who were persisting through college. The reason of why students who participated in the study were required to have completed 12 units (or at least four college courses) without a limit on time taken to complete the units was that students often leave college and come back for various reasons. This amount is the community college standard for a full-time student in one semester: this study just broadened the time requirement. This was based on the understanding that if a student left college and came back, this would show persistence and motivation to complete the associate's degree.

Study One Procedures

In collaboration with San Diego City College, a stratified sample of 30–40 students attending the college was developed. San Diego City College contacted the students via e-mail, faculty were e-mailed and asked to notify students in class, and fliers were placed around campus informing students of the proposed study. However, before any data was collected, I gained permission from San Diego City College's Institutional Review Board (IRB). While San Diego City College was sending the students information about the proposed study, I approached students on campus and attempted to gain their interest in the proposed study. Additionally, since I was a faculty member at the institution I was able to ask colleagues to announce the research and to arrange for participation to count as extra credit in their classes. As an advisor for a club, I was able to utilize the club's *Facebook* page to advertise the study. Before students were contacted, San Diego Community College IRB and I made sure that students met the criteria for the study. I recruited students for one week; after that week, potential participants could still contact me. After initial contact, I chose from the pool of interested participants and invited some to participate in the study. A confirmation e-mail was sent to participants, informing the students of the day, time, and location of the focus group. Focus groups were held for one week, one group a day, and for approximately one hour. At the time of the focus group, students were given an alias to protect their identity and before the interview began, I read the informed consent forms and explained the purpose of the study. Students signed the informed consent forms and received copies of the forms. Once the consent forms were signed and students had received copies, I began the interviews.

Recruitment

After approval from San Diego City College IRB and Argosy IRB, San Diego City College sent an e-mail to students who meet the criteria for the study and students contacted me directly if they were interested in the study. As noted above, I used social media as a means to recruit students. As an advisor for a club called *The Intellectual Roundtable*, I utilized the club's Facebook page to recruit students, and members were used to recruit students. Additionally, I asked colleagues to make an announcement in their classes informing students of the study. With each method of re-cruitment, a standard announcement was given or read to each student who was interested in the study. The announcement stated the dates and times that were available. This gave students an op-tion for the students to select the focus group session that they were able to attend, and this method was effective for ensuring students' availability. Lastly, fliers—which were the standard means of an-nouncement—were posted around the college. These requested that students contact me if interested in the study. These also provided a web link for student to read more about the study. This link was used as a means of confirming that students meet the criteria for the study.

Students who were interested in the study were eligible for a gift card ($50 value) as a thank you for participating in the study. The gift card was part of a raffle: the students wrote their e-mail address on the raffle ticket only as a contact for me to give the single winner of the raffle their prize after the study. The students were informed that participation will have no effect on their grades in classes. The recruitment was targeted at between 20–40 students for one focus group a week. Each focus group was planned two weeks in advanced, and recruitment continued during the waiting period. Once recruitment ended, students scheduled for the focus groups were sent the informed consent forms via e-mail: student brought signed informed consent forms to the scheduled focus group, and I made additional copies of the forms available on the day for students who forget to bring or sign consent forms.

San Diego City College IRB

I gathered and submitted the instrumentations, including informed consent forms, web-based informed consent forms, focus group questions, instruments, methods, and the approval of the Argosy University Internal Review Board (IRB) to gain permission from the San Diego Community College District to conduct research at

San Diego City College. The San Diego Community College District sent paperwork confirming the approval of the proposed research study. Afterwards, San Diego City College supplied a date to begin recruitment and permission to gather data. The college then assisted the research by sending an e-mail to students who were interested in participating in the proposed study. Additionally, the college assisted the research by sending informed consent forms via e-mail to students who wish to participate in the proposed study.

Focus Group: Interview

Interviews were conducted as on-campus focus group sessions. The participants were able to choose a focus group session based upon their availability and the focus group sessions were available throughout the week. E-mails were then sent to confirm students' participation in the focus group and to confirm that the students met the criteria of the study.

Instrumentation

Before beginning the process of gathering information, recruitment, and conducting focus groups, was paramount to gain Institutional Review Board (IRB) approval: "Researchers need to have their research plans reviewed by the (IRB) on their college and university campuses" (Creswell, 2009, p. 89). As noted above, no research was conducted until I had received approval from Argosy University IRB, San Diego City College IRB, and IRB institutions.

The instruments of the study were:

- Focus group questions
- Web-based survey questions, which were presented after the focus groups
- Informed consent form
- Web-based informed consent form

The students were asked ten research questions and the students shared their information through dialogue in the focus groups. As mentioned above, focus groups were held for only one week, with the days and times contingent upon participants' availability. An audio recording was made for each focus group session. The open-ended focus group questions were asked of students who meet the aforementioned criteria of the proposed study. As the students engaged in dialogue, my role was to ask the initial questions, listen, and finally to ask questions for further clarification to gain further information. This was based on an understanding that a researcher's role is to be involved and, at the same time, to not be involved (Krueger & Casey, 2000). After the focus group sessions, students were invited to participate in a web-based survey, which was presented after the focus groups had concluded. The web-based survey was used to validate the first study.

The ethics and the protection of the participants in any research study are always a concern for the researcher. Patton (2002) explained that the research study should not be covert: the research questions and purpose must have the consent of the participants in the study. The researcher is afforded protection by gaining written consent from the participants for the proposed study, so that each participant is well informed of the research processes and purpose of the proposed study (Patton, 2002). The information that the students shared was protected in this study, as were the students who participated in the study.

The concerns for the students and the data were communicated in the informed consent forms. The informed consent forms contained the details of ethical issues and the method by which the data was protected and stored to maintain confidentiality. Additionally, the informed consent forms included the purpose of the proposed study, the environment, and the role of participants. The informed consent forms served to provide a written form of acknowledgement of ethics and confidentiality. I also verbally reviewed and explained the contents of the informed consent form before each focus group session began. The information provided by the participants was protected through storage in a laptop computer with a password that I knew, and after one year the information from the study this data will be destroyed.

Diction 6.0 Content Text Analysis Software

Utilizing a *Windows* platform, Diction 6.0 is a context text analysis program that is coded for certainty and commonality (Lowe, n.d.):

> Certainty: Language indicating resoluteness, inflexibility, and completeness and a tendency to speak ex-cathedra; Activity: Language featuring movement, change, the implementation of ideas and the avoidance of inertia; Optimism: Language endorsing some person, group, concept or event or highlighting their positive entailments; Commonality: Language highlighting the agreed-upon values of a group and rejecting idiosyncratic modes of engagement; Realism: Language describing tangible, immediate, recognizable matters that affect people's everyday lives (p. 6).

After the focus group sessions were completed, I used the program Diction 6.0 to create themes and categorize the responses from the students. I then used the responses from the students to create the questions for the web-based survey.

Content Analysis

Once the data was gathered from the 30–40 student participants, I used the process of content analysis to analyze the data. The purpose of using content analysis for this proposed study was to understand students' experiences and to understand how those experiences motivated students. Patton (2002) explained this approach as a naturalistic inquiry, qualitative data, and statistical analysis. Denzin stated:

Naturalists inspect and organize behavior specimens in ways which they hope will permit them to progressively reveal and better understand the underlying problematic features of the social world under study. They seek to ask the question or set of questions which will make that world or social organization understandable (cited in Patton, 2002, p. 470).

The naturalist approach was used while conducting the focus groups. The analysis of data gathered in the focus groups was transcript-based because: "Transcript-based analysis uses unabridged transcripts of the focus groups as a basis for analysis. These are often supplemented with field notes taken by the researcher" (Krueger & Casey, 2000, p. 130). Computers were used to analyze the data for the following reason: "QDA [qualitative data analysis] programs improve our work by removing drudgery in managing qualitative data. Copying, highlighting, cross-referencing, cutting and pasting transcripts and field notes" (Patton, 2002, p. 442). This use of QDA was crucial, because analyzing community college students' responses through the language used by students identified themes, commonalities, and patterns among college students.

The data collected from Diction 6.0 formed the basis for the quantitative portion of the proposed study, which was the statistical analysis. The web-based survey was cross-sectional (Creswell, 2009), correlating with the data from the focus groups. The purpose of the web-based survey was "to generalize from a sample to a population so that inferences can be made about some characteristic, attitude, or behavior of this population" (Creswell, 2009, p. 146). In this study, the population was college students and interpretation of student motivation was the characteristic being examined.

Study Two: Web-Based Survey

Utilizing a web-based survey to quantify the data allowed me to "generalize from a sample to a population so that inferences can be made about some characteristic, attitude, or behavior of this population" (Creswell, 2009, p. 146). The information from the focus groups allowed the use of Diction 6.0 to create themes and categories that developed additional questions for the web-based survey. The web-based survey was used to either validate or invalidate the information from the focus groups. Thereby, as Creswell (2009) noted, "whether the survey will be cross-sectional, with the data collected at one point in time" (p. 146). This research study used a comparison cross-sectional between college students' intrinsic motivation, college students' choice to attend college, and college students' efficacy. The web-based survey quantified students' responses from the focus groups and validated the information.

Sample Size

In collaboration with San Diego City College, I surveyed approximately 100 students for the quantitative portion (study two of the research). Creswell (2002) outlined an ideal range for sampling: "If there are 1,000 people, 278 people must be sampled (28%), and if there are 5,000 people in the population of interest, 357 must be sampled (7%) to achieve a 95% confidence" (p. 245). This was adopted as a benchmark for the study.

Instrumentation

The web-based survey used a set of questions pertaining to the themes of the focus group. The survey consisted of a 5-point Likert scale to identify if a universal consensus existed. Rensis Likert (1973) identified that the Likert scale is used to measure characteristics of an organization. For this study, the scale measured college students' motivation with respect to enrolling and staying in an educational organization. Likert further noted:

> Likert identifies three sets of variables: (1) causal variables, factors controlled by managers—such as organizational struc-

ture, controls, policies, and leadership behavior; (2) intervening variables—the attitudes, motivations, and perceptions of all the members; (3) the end-result variables, factors such as productivity, costs, and profits (p. 33).

Surveys can provide a type of quantitative data, which allow the researcher to find trends, patterns, and commonalities between students' motivations. I used the data from the focus group to find trends through a comparative analysis. This cross-sectional survey served to compare other students' motivations and to identify whether other students shared the same experience.

The web-based survey contained the same information that was gained in the focus groups. The 5-point Likert scale was used to further define what motivates students, and consisted of the following items: *1 (strongly agree), 2 (agree), 3 (neutral), 4 (disagree), and 5 (strongly disagree).*

STUDY TWO PROCEDURES

Development of Web-Based Survey Questions

The web-based survey consisted of closed-ended questions based on the themes from the answers provided by the focus groups. Diction 6.0 software was used to create and develop themes for the online survey, which consisted of fifteen questions. Before the web-based survey was available, informed consent forms were sent to potential participants, and the survey became available to them once they had signed and agreed to the consent form. San Diego City College was the primary distributor of the online survey information to the students. The respondents received log-in information, confidentiality agreement, and right to withdraw notice. The latter was important, because participants had the right to know and to terminate themselves from the proposed study at any time without consequence (Creswell, 2009). The purpose of this survey was to validate or invalidate the responses of the focus group, thereby aiding in the cross-reference analysis.

Study Two: SDCCD Web-Based Surveys

The web-based survey was conducted with San Diego City College for the second portion of the study. The survey instruments consisted of a questionnaire with 15 questions derived from the responses of the focus groups and themes developed by Diction 6.0. I used the responses to the closed-ended questions to explore any intersections with the qualitative data. This comparative cross-section revealed themes that were not identified in the focus groups.

Once approval was received from Argosy University, San Diego City College, and IRB Institution, participants were given time before actually taking the online survey and they were notified of the dates that the survey was available. An e-mail was sent to all potential participants provided by the college stating that the survey would be accessible to the participants for 30 days.

Consent Forms E-Mailed

Once the IRB and San Diego City College had approved study two, the college e-mailed an announcement to students informing students that the survey and informed consent forms were available online. Students had the ability to terminate their participation in the study without penalty at any time during the survey.

Recruitment

As part one in the study, recruitment did not begin until approval of San Diego City College IRB and Argosy IRB was received. San Diego City College—as in study one—sent an e-mail to students who fit the criteria of the study. Students were recruited from other community colleges, such as Grossmont College, Cuyamaca College, Southwestern College, Mesa College, and Mira Mar College (these covered the community colleges in San Diego) for the second part of the study to quantify the data and validate study one. No recruitment began begin until IRB approval was received for each college. As a primary method to recruit students, each college sent e-mails to students who meet the criteria of the study. Students were given a web link in the e-mail to the web-based survey. This link was provided by a global consortium, which had a secure online database wherein students could take the online survey. Similar to in study one, The Intellectual Roundtable's Facebook webpage was used to recruit students. Furthermore, students who participated in the focus groups were invited to participate in the web-based survey. As in study one, students had a chance to win a $50 dollar gift card in a raffle, thus students were required to provide their e-mail address for me to contact the single winner of their prize. Also similar to study one, participants were informed that the online survey would have no impact on their classes, and that e-mail addresses would only be used to contact the winner of the raffle.

Assumptions

Focus group inquiry explores how people really think and feel by allowing them to communicate with each other about similar situations (Kruegar & Casey, 2000). The assumptions that I had were the reason for conducting this study that serves to increase the level of inquiry about students' motivations. My assumptions were:

1. Students may not know their own identity.
2. Students may not understand what motivates them.
3. Students may not understand their own efficacy.
4. Each student will have different sets of values that will influence his/her persistence.
5. I will be able to give ample time for each student.

6. Each student will be able to articulate his/her own factors of persistence.
7. Diction 6.0 will be able to measure emotions, patterns, and themes of the student responses.
8. Not every student will be comfortable with sharing their experiences or stating how this affects their persistence for college.
9. Not every invited student will participate.

Chapter Four

Findings

The research identified factors that influenced the motivation of students in the net generation to stay in college. This chapter presents the findings and provides a summary of the research. The information is organized into the following sections: restatement of the purpose, data collection procedures, data analysis, and summary of interview questions.

RESTATEMENT OF THE PROBLEM

The purpose of the study was to develop a conceptual framework to empower educational institutions to retain students and allow students to persist through education.

DATA COLLECTION PROCEDURES

Researcher's Data Collection Experience

The research design utilized a mixed methods approach. As noted in the previous chapter, Creswell (2009) clarified that the mixed methods approach is a combination of qualitative and quantitative research methods. This approach, by not adhering to one method, benefits from both research methodologies. In the research design, the initial stage involved conducting focus groups. During the first phase of recruitment, the San Diego City College sent notification to the students who fitted the stratified sample. These students then emailed the researcher to express interest in participating in the study. However, the participant's schedules conflicted, making it difficult to gather sufficient numbers to conduct a focus group. For this reason, the research design was changed to use one-on-one interviews.

Participants

The participants were students from San Diego City College who fitted the stratified sample of this study. The sample for this initial stage of the study consisted of a total 25 participants: 20 female and 5 male (80% female and 20% male).

DATA ANALYSIS

The purpose of this study was to explore the factors that motivate students of the net generation to stay in college. The objective of this analysis was to answer the following research questions:

1. How do students develop their identity in college?
2. Why do students choose to attend college?
3. How successful are students in college?

Step 1: Open-Ended One-on-One Interviews

The one-on-one interviews were designed to underscore the theories discussed in the review of literature. Questions 1–3 supported the theoretical framework of identity development (Intrinsic Motivation); questions 4–6 and 8 supported the context of choice theory (Education), and questions 7 and 9 informed the theory of self-efficacy (College Student Persistence). After the one-on-one interviews were conducted and recorded, the responses were transcribed using *Transcription Star* services. The resulting data was then manually encoded into themes to compare and contrast the individual participants in relation to the group. The themes were manually derived from reviewing the interview transcriptions and noting patterns of consistency and similarities in the discussions. The data was manually encoded into two different formats for further clarify the themes. The first coding of the data highlighted any recurring responses, word-for-word, to show the strength of the theme. In this way, the responses of each participant were tallied according to their content. The second encoding used the word-for-word statements of participants as the basis for identifying the core message. This was used to develop each theme. The information from the developed themes provided.

Once these themes were developed and clarified, they become the basis for the web-based survey. The qualitative phase provided the themes, which facilitated the emergence of data for the second or quantitative phase (Creswell, 2009).

SUMMARY OF INTERVIEW QUESTIONS

The first question used in the study was: "What is your major?" This question was used as an opening 'icebreaker' question. The purpose of this question was to place the participant at ease and as such it was not used in the study to create themes. Therefore, for the purposes of this study, question 1 was considered to be: "Who do you socialize with in college?"

Questions 1–3 identified the development and intrinsic motivation of students. Questions 4–6 and 8 revealed education and examined choice theory, while questions 7 and 9 showed the college students' persistence and examined the theory of self-efficacy (as shown in Table 4.1). The interview questions were designed to answer the research questions and reflect the three theories used in the review of literature.

Table 4.1.   Manually-encoded Data

Interview Question	Themes Developed
1	a. Quality/level of intimacy b. Characteristics of people
2	a. Personal growth b. Self-knowledge
3	a. Environmental influences or external control of change b. Individual control of internal control of change
4	a. Future plans b. Social influences c. Time of decision
5	a. Learning standards to gain career or job of choice b. Learning about self c. Achieving goal
6	a. Social support b. Financial support c. Self-supportive
7	a. Achieve goals
8	a. Most influential b. Comfortable lifestyle
9	a. Type of support b. Need for support

Step 2: Content Text Analysis Using Diction 6.0

Diction 6.0 is a content text analysis program that was used in this study as a tool to understand the meaning of the responses, patterns, and themes from the one-on-one interviews. The results from Diction 6.0 provided a set of *outliers*: outliers reflect the extreme positive and negative side on a bell curve. The outliers were based on the dictionaries provided by the Diction 6.0 software. These outliers consisted of a set of words that allowed an organized meaning to be identified from the transcribed content of each interview.

Master Variables

Diction 6.0 uses five *master variables*. These five master variables, "when taken together… provide the most general understanding of a given text." The five master variables for this study were constructed by "concatenating 31 dictionary scores." Not every subcategory was present in this calculation, as those that did not reflect the participant's responses were found either to be absent or to produce a value that was too low to determine effectively.

The first variable that was identified using Diction 6.0 was Certainty. The software as defined this variable: "Language indicating resoluteness, inflexibility, and completeness and a tendency to speak ex cathedra." The two questions where Certainty did not emerge were Question 3 ("What influenced you to change your personality in college?") and Question 5 ("What is the benefit of staying in college, short and long term?"). However, Certainty fell into the low normative values for the rest of the questions. Thus, participants were not certain when asked the two (out of three) questions pertaining to identity (research question 1). For three of the four questions that concerned education (research question 2), the participants showed a low normative value of Certainty. For the question of how successful students were in college (research question 3), responses to both questions about college student persistence showed a low level of Certainty.

The second variable that was identified using Diction 6.0 was Optimism. Diction 6.0 defined this as: "Language endorsing some person, group, and concept or highlighting their positive entailments." The variable of Optimism emerged in every question except Question 6 ("Do you have a support system to stay in college?"). Aside from this latter question, Optimism was associated with a high normative value in every question asked about the factor of staying in college. In response to the questions relating to how students develop their identity in college (research question 1), the participants were Optimistic about being motivated intrinsically. The college students were Optimistic about their decision to attend college (research question 2): showing a high value of Optimism for three out of four questions asked about education. Finally, the participants showed high levels of Optimism in response to questions relating to success in college (research question 3) and therefore were optimistic about their ability to persist in college.

The third variable that was identified using Diction 6.0 was Commonality. Diction 6.0 defined Commonality as: "Language highlighting the agreed-upon values of a group and rejecting idiosyncratic modes of engagement." Commonality only emerged once within of the questions pertaining to why students stay in college: this was in Question 2 ("Has your personality changed in college and how?"). The participants revealed high normative value for this question, thus showing a Commonality pertaining to students and education.

Results for Question 1

Question 1 asked the participants about the people they chose to socialize with in college. Of the five Master Variables, three are shown. Below the master variables of certainty, optimism, and commonality were two different subcategories: these were identified as outliers, and thus were both above the normative value. These two subcategories were Self-reference (high) and Satisfaction (high). These were the only two subcategories with high normative ranges in every question.

The first outlier determined by Diction 6.0 from Question 1 was Self-reference. According to Diction 6.0, Self-reference responses "are treated as acts of indexing whereby the locus of action appears to reside in the speaker and not in the world at large thereby implicitly acknowledge the speaker's limited vision." Examples of Self-reference include words such as "I, I will, I would, or I am." The responses from the participants that reflected this definition included statements such as "I socialize with my friends well, I so-

cialize with the students in class and I also talk to the teachers";
"My friends, my sister is also attending the same school as me right
now, so my sister. I meet a lot of new people"; and "I socialize with
a lot of different kinds of people... I mostly associate myself with
my friends who have their lives together and obviously that kind of
drifted off from the people who just want to party." Participants
showed Self-reference by stating, "I meet" and "I socialize with."
The responses to Question 1 ranged high above normal, which
showed that participants evidenced Self-reference while being social; when students discussed socializing in college, they refer-
enced themselves by using "I."

The second outlier determined by Diction 6.0 from Question 1
was Satisfaction. Diction 6.0 defined Satisfaction as "positive affective states with moments of undiminished joy, and pleasurable
diversion." An example of Satisfaction is an emotional or affective
state: such as "cheerful, excited, fun, or thanks." Satisfaction from
the participants was apparent in statements such as "My friends or
anybody else that I meet. It could be a random day and I can meet
somebody new, just say hello and try to make somebody's day";
"Yeah. My family, my coworkers... I work [often at] home. So I
hang out, my coworkers there. Few friends from, like, high
school"; and "Most of the time, I'm trying to witness to people,
'cause I'm blessed by the Lord: that he brings me to focus on who
He is and [in] school to keep going, to move on." In these examples, participants show Satisfaction when they make another person
happy ("try to make somebody's day") or when they state that, they
prefer to socialize ("So I hang out with my coworkers there").
These statements show high levels of Satisfaction with socializing
in college: thus, these statements show that the students in college
are satisfied with the people with whom they are socializing.

Results for Question 2

Question 2 asked the participants if their personality had changed in college, and asked them to specify how. Of the three master variables (Certainty, Optimism, and Commonality), five different subcategories were identified as outliers, and each subcategory was above the normative value. The five subcategories outside of normative range were Ambivalence (high), Self-reference (high), Tenacity (high), Satisfaction (high), and Cooperation (high).

Ambivalence was shown in "words expressing hesitation or uncertainty, implying a speaker's inability or unwillingness to commit to the verbalization being made" (Diction 6.0), example words to depict Ambivalence include "almost, could, and suppose." Participants with personality changes in college showed Ambivalence with responses such as: "I don't know, my personality is always kind of up and down"; "I don't think it's really changed" and "I don't know. I don't think so; kind of the same." Responses from the participants revealed high levels of Ambivalence. Thus, students of the net-generation are uncertain or do not know if their personality has changed in college (evidenced, for example, in the statements "I don't think it's changed" and "I don't know").

Participants expressed Self-reference in this question with verbalizations such as "So it's pushing me to be more mature, it's pushed me to be overall better. I can't say, I'm not going to say that I see myself as a better person than the rest, but I think I am definitely better than the person I was a year ago"; "I have more knowledge now, so that may have affected what I like: my choices and my perspective. A little bit more self-sufficient. Actually, yeah, I talk more"; and "More motivated because in high school we didn't really care, and in high school I'm actually trying more." Responses from participants showed high levels of Self-reference when asked how their personalities had changed in college. The use of "I" shows that students acknowledge their personality in college.

Tenacity was identified in the responses with the "verb to be (*is, am, will, shall*), three definitive verb forms (*has, must, do*) and their variants, as well as all associated contractions (*he'll, they've, ain't*). These verbs connote confidence and totality." Participants expressed Tenacity with responses such as: "College has been a big step for me because it's pushed me to be more independent"; "I'll have all my credits, all my units, all my things lined up for whatever I wanna do." Moreover, added to this was the Tenacity of the participants while in college: "My personality has changed—I think I can say I've matured more, 'cause now I realize, like, this is it; like, this is, like, my next step to live and so I have to get my things straight and I think I've grown up since then." These participants revealed high levels of Tenacity through the use of statements "I'll have" and "I've matured": the students were not giving up or quitting. This language of Tenacity was evident when college students of the net generation experienced changes to their personality.

Participants revealed Satisfaction in this question with statements such as: "It has been awesome you know, it's opened this whole new world for me and I love it and I enjoy school, it is awesome"; "I don't think it's changed. I just think it enhanced it. I've always had this extraverted, open, bubbly, personality"; and "Just wasn't ready. Um and then, so this is my second time giving it a go." Satisfaction is shown to be high in the statements: "it is awesome" and "always has this extraverted, open, bubbly, personality." This high level of Satisfaction shows that students of the net generation are happy about their personality changes in college.

Diction 6.0 defined Cooperation as: "Terms designating behavioral interactions among people that often result in a group product." Examples of Cooperation include "schoolmates, friendship, or teamwork." Participants showed Cooperation in their responses to this question: "I've to fend for myself so that helps me, like, build relationships with classmates and stuff because I know that's how

I'm going to get through"; "Yeah the school helps to because, like, I had physical problems for a while, so then the help services the disability help services really helps… [also helpful is] talking to professors" and "When I was with my family there was a lot of things that I had to do on my own, like, take care of my bother when my mom was gone or take care of my dad when he was sick, so there was a lot of maturity involved in growing up." These statements show Cooperation, which participants evidenced at high levels. Phrases such as "building relationships" and "take care of my dad" showed that the participants were able to work with or care for others. This suggests that college students of the net-generation cite Cooperation when their personality changes in college.

Results for Question 3

Question 3 asked the participants about what influenced them to change their personality in college. Of the three master variables, four different subcategories were identified as outliers, and all of these were above normative value. The subcategories outside of normative range were Ambivalence (high), Self-reference (high), Tenacity (high), and Satisfaction (high).

Ambivalence was shown in responses such as: "I don't think my personality has changed"; "I don't know, it's just, I don't know"; and "I don't know—maybe moving here." The high levels of Ambivalence were evidenced, for example, by the response of "I don't know" when a participant was asked about the influences that changed the net-generation student's personality in college.

Participants expressed Self-reference in this question by verbalizing the following: "I felt like I've conquered a little bit of my procrastination tendencies and a little bit of my laziness. I still have a lot that I need to work on but—"; "Yeah, and I'm extrovert, actually"; and "I've always wanted to prove my dad wrong because he is really what changed me." Participants showed high levels of Self-reference by referring to themselves using "I." This suggests that students of the net generation refer to themselves when considering an influence of changing their personality.

Participants evidenced high Tenacity, with some of the responses as follows: "They become somebody that they don't wanna be, so I chose not to change the personality because I am who I am and I don't wanna change it because somebody told me to change it"; "I don't think my personality has changed, just my motivation and drive has just excelled"; and "Well, many of the teachers I have had, I have had great teachers. Awesome teachers and they rubbed off on me and, they've inspired me and, they've made me believe that no dream is too big, and they've supported me." Examples of Tenacity in these statements include "don't wanna" and "they've inspired me." The results reveal high levels of Tenacity when students of the net generation describe the influences that changed their personality in college.

Participants revealed high levels of Satisfaction in this question. Responses included "Well, many of the teachers I have had, I have had great teachers. Awesome teachers and they rubbed off on me and, they've inspired me and, they've made me believe that no dream is too big, and they've supported me. I mean it has been a great experience"; "So, that motivates you to be somewhere every day on time and I really like doing this internship. So, to me it doesn't feel like work, it feels like this is fun, I'm learning things that I like to learn. I do it for free, you know, it's [an] internship"; and "I guess just all the information I was learning and some of the professors, very [much] encouraged [us]. Students are expressing that they are satisfied or happy with the influence for their personality to change in college. Encouraging, yeah." Words of Satisfaction that were used here include "great teachers" and "this is fun." These students are expressing that they are satisfied or happy with the influence for their personality to change in college.

Results for Question 4

Question 4 asked the participants when they decided to go to college. Of the three master variables, three different subcategories were identified as outliers, and all were above normative value. The three subcategories outside of normative range in this question were Self-reference (high), Praise (high), and Satisfaction (high).

Participants expressed Self-reference by verbalizing statements such as: "I graduated in 2007, high school. So I took a year off, didn't know what I wanted to do, got in college, just knew that I needed to go to school"; "During high school. I mean, at first I was just like I shouldn't go. I was just so caught up with my friend you can say, but I motivated her to go because I knew I didn't want to leave her behind"; and "So I'm like yeah, I'm just going to go straight to college, I'm not going to do the military thing. Everyone in my family is military and I'm like no, no, I can do the school, I hope I do that." The language of "I" shows Self-reference. These results revealed high levels of Self-reference, suggesting that students of the net generation generally decided to go to college by themselves.

The subcategory of Praise is defined within Diction 6.0 as:

> Affirmations of some person, group, or abstract entity. Included are terms isolating important social qualities (*dear, delightful, witty*), physical qualities (*mighty, handsome, beautiful*), intellectual qualities (*shrewd, bright, vigilant, reasonable*), entrepreneurial qualities (*successful, conscientious, renowned*), and moral qualities (*faithful, good, noble*). All terms in this dictionary are adjectives.

Responses that evidenced Praise included: "Ever since I was little, my mom was saying 'you're the one who has [to] take care of me,' so, I always knew [that I would be] taking care of my parents, and I am [cap]able"; "I've always wanted to go to college. I was kind of that kid growing up in school who always like raised their hands and answers and I've got good grades all through primary school and stuff. So, I've always wanted to go but I was lazy and I had to work"; and "No, not really, just that's kind of what was said I was going to do and I had no choice, which I mean I didn't really mind. I like going to school in the sense that I like I fell like it's actually I'm doing something and I don't mind learning. So it occupies my time and it's something good to occupy my time with, so." Examples of Praise in these responses include "I am able" and "I've got good grades." Participants responded with high levels of Praise, which shows that Praise influenced the decisions of students from the net generation to go to college.

Participants revealed high levels of Satisfaction, with students expressing that they were satisfied with the decision made to go to college: "I decided to go to college right after high school because I didn't want to—because I didn't want to just like, just not, not to stay at home"; "'There's nothing wrong with community college,' and everyone has that negative stigma towards community college but I don't see why we're saving money. I don't pay $20,000 for a couple of classes. I'm getting a full load for $500.00. So, the professors here are amazing. I always have a love for this campus because they enforce community"; and "Yeah, my mom is always like 'oh, you should be a doctor, you should be like and go straight go to college' … yeah it's an influence." Participants showed satisfaction by being happy about being independent ("not to stay at home") and expressing contentment about their choice ("There's nothing wrong with a community college"). In this way, net-generation students show satisfaction or happiness about their decision as to when they to go to college.

Results for Question 5

Question 5 asked the participants about the benefits of staying in college, both in the short term and in the long term. Of the three master variables, four different subcategories were identified as outliers, and all were above normative value. The four subcategories outside of normative range were Ambivalence (high), Self-reference (high), Tenacity (high), and Satisfaction (high).

Ambivalence was indicated in the following statements: "I think... I think this is like another it depends on your perspective for me"; "I think mostly my view is all like, I look at it mostly long term I haven't really thought of it as a short term before" and "Ah-hmm. I never, I don't, I don't know. I don't really ever think of short term." Participants showed high levels of Ambivalence in relation to the benefits of staying in college in both short and long term. Examples of the students' Ambivalence in these statements included in: "I think this is like another it depends on your perspective" and "I haven't really thought of it as a short term before." These suggest that the students either do not know, or have not thought about, the benefits of staying in college.

Self-reference in this question can be identified in statements such as: "Long-term, I will be able to very established, I won't have to worry so much about money if I get in a good position, and I can get a house one day, have kids, all that stuff. Short-term, it occupies my time, it's a good experience, I feel like you get to grow. I do feel like in a sense I am kind of really getting to know me better and I like the experience of it"; "Short term is I learn a lot of things. I don't realize it but it helps me: like, I learn one thing in one class and then I see it in all my other classes and I make a lot of friends and they kind of formulate support systems. And then long term I'll eventually make more money when this is all over with hoping"; and "Long-term goal will be transferring to the university. Transfer to University. I have to finish. Well, for myself, just knowing that my success—I always wanted to be higher than my parents, well, they always told me I'm gonna be higher than them." Students refer to themselves when this pertains to the benefit of staying in college (short and long term). Students reveal high levels of self-reference, specifically, when they state: "I'll eventually make more money" and "I always wanted to be higher than my parents." These are personal reasons that acknowledge the benefit of staying in college for both short and long term.

Participants expressed high levels of Tenacity in this question. Some of the responses are as follows: "Probably so. I must, if I knew for sure I didn't have to go to school to be successful, I don't know, I think I still would go to school, probably like—because I have decided just go for myself"; "Long-term, I will be able to very established, I won't have to worry so much about money if I get in a good position, and I can get a house one day, have kids, all that stuff"; and "Short-term I would say I'm growing a lot still and I'm acquiring knowledge from a lot of subfields, so that's what I would say short-term. Long-term, I will know a lot about a certain subject and I would be able to share it with the community." In these responses, students indicated that in college that they were not giving up, as they recognized the benefit of staying in college. Examples of Tenacity in the responses are "I must, if I knew for sure I didn't have to go to school to be successful" and "I won't have to worry about money." These show that students desire to achieve their goals and that this this is the benefit of staying in college in both the short and long terms.

Participants revealed high levels of Satisfaction in this question, expressing that they were satisfied with the short and long term benefits of staying in college. Participants stated the following: "Long term, I'm just hoping that instead of spending, like, so much time working up, up, up, up in a business, that trying really hard in school and actually absorbing it may really, like help me apply it all to real life. So that if (and when) I do get hired, it'll be a faster process: it'll be easier and [there will] be way more opportunities I think. So, I'm excited about that part."; "Short term would be the enjoyment of learning"; and "Short-term I could say basically learning what you wanna do, being inside classes makes me look at more things, I could say, that's the short term and, like, the education, I love education, so that's what really gets me going." Satisfaction was revealed to be high, for example, with "I'm excited" and "I love education." Overall, this result indicates that students show satisfaction about the benefits of staying in college for the short and long terms.

Results for Question 6

Question 6 asked the participants about the presence of a support system to assist them with staying in college. Of the three master variables, four different subcategories were identified as outliers, and all were above normative value. The four subcategories outside of normative range in this question were Self-reference (high), Tenacity (high), Satisfaction (high), and Denial (high).

Self-reference was evident in the following responses to this question: "I guess the Navy, I get funds. The Navy pays for—well right now, I'm not using the funding from the military but I do have the Board of Governor's Grant, and then for the next three years I'm going to be using the Navy's"; "Well my uncle is the one which helps a lot. I mean I do pay rent but it is really low, so that really helps"; and "I have an extremely well-rounded support system. My uncle and my aunt are very into my education. They've always been." Self-reference was high, as shown in such phrases as "I guess the Navy" and "I mean I do pay rent," which both show a relation to self. This result indicates that students of the net generation have a support system to stay in college by relating back to self.

Participants expressed high levels of Tenacity in this question. Some of the responses are as follows: "I kept that distance from school, like I would come to my classes and go home and live my life you know and now it has been the opposite. Now I have kind of like immersed myself into school, you know I have got together with teachers, students from school and kind of left like that whole set of friends you know behind"; "So, I will now be able to get financial aid. However, for the past two and a half years that I've been to college, I haven't gotten any. So, it's been really tough"; and "I have just recently had to do that with a couple of my friends who, you know, I cherish our friendship but they are not students and so they just distracting me on the weekends and when I'm supposed to be studying." Tenacity was exemplified through phrases such as: "I will be able" and "I have just recently." These show the students' willingness to not give up and to continue. These results suggest that students of the net generation have an effective support system in college.

Participants revealed high levels of Satisfaction. The students expressed that they were satisfied with the personality change that was happening to them in college with the following statements: "I have a great non-material support system my family, my friends, my work they all really respect actually I try really that I love school I try really hard financial support system is definitely at a low but I'm making it and it'll be worth it in the end"; "Yeah, I would say family members and like I said before the teachers and stuff I've been able to kind of lean on them, it's been awesome"; and "Yes. My mom is the greatest: her thing being, she supports me now and I support her later. So, like, I have free rent. I pay for my own food, but, I mean, I have her support and her love, so that's all I need." Satisfaction was revealed as high through language such as: "I have a great non-material support system" and "kind of lean on them, it's been awesome" showing students excitement, and happiness about their support system. This suggests that students of the net generation are satisfied, and that and this support system will support them to stay in college.

Results for Question 7

Question 7 asked the participants about their plans to stay next year and their reasons for these plans. Of the three master variables, two different subcategories were identified as outliers, and all were above normative value. The two subcategories outside of normative range were Self-reference (high) and Satisfaction (high).

Self-reference was shown in statements such as: "Yeah, because I have to finish. Yes I will stay in school next year until I am done, you know, I cannot wait till I am done" and "Yes. I'm planning to stay in school next year because I'm planning to transfer, so, right now I'm just doing my generals, and then to see, like, then—my transfer requirements for my major later on. I'm going to stay in school next year just because I want to hurry up and transfer, and I'd like to get a degree so I can get a good job as soon as I can." In this way, participants explained that the reason for their plans to stay in college next year were related to interests of self. The participants showed Self-reference by stating: "Yeah, because I have to finish" and "I want to hurry up and transfer." The results showed high levels of Self-reference in relation to their plans to stay in college for the next year.

Participants revealed high levels of Satisfaction in relation to this question. Students expressed that they were satisfied in the decision to return to college the next year with statements such as: "Yeah, and even when I plan on after I get my degree and stuff I planning coming back to school to doing more of the fun stuff I want to. I've always wanted to take some art classes, some of the sport classes even. I always want to kind of look into the mechanical class and I thought that would be fun ... there is not enough time right now, and I need to get a job right now, so that's what I'm doing just kind of focusing on that goal"; "Yeah support and it will just be awesome, you know, new experience and really focused on school"; and "Of course. Because I love learning and I love growing." Participants explained that they planned to stay in college next year as they were accomplishing what they want to achieve. Participants showed Satisfaction by stating: "Yeah and even what I plan on after I get my degree and stuff I'm planning coming back to school" and "Because I love learning and I love growing." Satisfaction was thus high as it pertained to staying in school next year.

Results of Question 8

Question 8 asked the participants about who influenced them the most in their decision to go to college. Of the three master variables, three different subcategories were identified as outliers, and all were above normative value. The three subcategories were Self-reference (high), Praise (high), and Satisfaction (high).

Self-reference was shown to be at a high level for this question. Examples of Self-reference in the responses to this question include: "I think I influenced myself. My parents wanted me to go to college, but influencing me so much, I don't think they were a big influence because they didn't go to college"; "I can say my mom for one, my dad. Before he passed, he told me, I mean, to make sure I have an education to get where I wanna be in life or anything like that"; and "Yeah kind of I mean as far as my place in the world I'm not really I'm not sure it's like a destiny thing I'm not really into a destiny thing, I'm just kind of doing what feels right and just kind of living life but not living life where I'm just like 'oh, I'm going to just go have fun all the time,' because that doesn't really work." The language of self-reference is apparent in phrases such as, "I think I influenced myself" and "I can say my mom," as each of these statements relates to self. Net-generation students, when asked who influenced them the most to go to college, referred to mostly to themselves.

The subcategory of Praise was shown to be high in relation to this question. Examples of responses that contributed to this include, "My uncle. He pushed me to go to school and so I was okay. I go to school"; "Mom. I know that's weird but like as I said she pushed me like stay in school be smart, you are smart you're getting good grades like ever since you were like to obviously not too like you know what I mean"; and "I think all my life she just wanted me she has always wanted me to do good in school and do something." The language of self-reference is shown in "you are smart" and "she has always wanted me to do good in school and do something": as each of these statements relates to a positive quality about the individual. This suggests that net-generation students were likely to praise the individual for the influence.

Participants revealed high levels of Satisfaction for this question. Students expressed that they were satisfied with the personality change that was happening to them in college: "I just saw them going to college and like being out there and having like a life and I was just like working, you know it's not working for me, you know it's just like I need it, like I wanted to have fun too, I want to go to school. I don't want just be like stuck working for the rest of my life"; "I just want to go to college because I knew I love school basically I like school so I want to stay in school, so…"; and "you are really going to thrive there and you are going to do really good, and I was like, okay. Thanks. So that helped." The language of Satisfaction is shown in: "I wanted to have fun too, I want to go to school" and "I was like, okay. Thanks. So that helped," as in each statement the student was positive about their experience in college. This shows that net-generation students, when asked who influenced them the most to go to college, expressed that they were satisfied with the influence.

Results for Question 9

Question 9 asked the participants about their support system for succeeding in college. Of the three master variables, four different subcategories were identified as outliers, and all were above normative value. The four subcategories outside of normative range were Ambivalence (high), Self-reference (high), Satisfaction (high), and Denial (high).

Ambivalence was high in the question. This was apparent in statements such as "Yeah, I know. It's just like, you would say my mom, she is, like, the motivation, the, you could say, the key of why I do certain things too"; "No, I don't think so. I'm trying to think it's high to think of like on my paths on the spot. I think really just the whole thing with the right out of my high school is like my biggest thought is like it's really good to kind of have like that real life experience right before you go into college because I value everything a lot more now"; and "I think managing my time well but I procrastinate too much." The language of Ambivalence can be seen in: "No, I don't think so" and "I think managing my time well," as each statement refers uncertainty or not knowing. These results indicate that students of the net generation have a support system to help them succeed in college, but this system is either unknown or not they are not sure of the support.

Self-reference was shown to be high for this question. Examples of statements that indicate Self-reference include: "Are treated as acts of indexing whereby the locus of action appears to reside in the speaker and not in the world at large thereby implicitly acknowledge the speaker's limited vision"; "No, because if I didn't have a support system I—it's not going to stop me from doing what I want to do"; "And then myself, definitely myself. For me, it's really— it's hard. School is hard for me. It's really, really hard and I have like an attention span of—well, I just get distracted very easily and, uhmm, and, but I have to—I have many conversations with myself [laughing] all the times so I'm a big factor as well"; and "I think your biggest support system has to be yourself because no one else can motivate you. So, generally I think it is me, because I'm the one that has to tell myself, go sit down go to the tutor, get your work done. And if I can't make, get the willpower to tell myself this is what you are going to do and you have to do it, it doesn't matter who else tells me. So I feel like it really starts with me and then having other friends who try hard saying you can do it or I, you know, because I tend to be the one that pushes other people." The language of Self-reference is apparent in phrases such as "I didn't have a support system" and "And then myself, definitely myself. For me, it's really—it's hard." Each statement refers back to the individual or self. These results indicate that net-generation students use their support system to help them succeed in college for reasons related to self.

Participants evidenced high levels of Satisfaction for this question. The students expressed that they were satisfied with the personality change that was happening to them in college: "And then calling my dad and asking him to give me, like, some kind of happy vibes cause sometimes I'm in a dark place and I need…"; "I would say probably just my family, my work and my friends they are I think like succeeding in school is highly respected so it's encouraging to have people to be like oh, look what I did I guess choosy as it is it is really important for someone to care someone to support you or I encourage you more"; and "So it's, I think my next step is I am going to look at the college that I want to go to and really see what they are expecting and try to do more community service because maybe that will help get me back into the whole, yeah, motivation." Examples to show language of Satisfaction are "some kind of happy vibes" and "so it's encouraging to have people": each statement shows a joy or happiness of the student. These results indicate that students of the net generation are satisfied with support system that is helping them succeed in college.

The responses to this question showed high levels of Denial. Diction 6.0 defined Denial as: "A dictionary consisting of standard negative contractions (*aren't, shouldn't, don't*), negative functions words (*nor, not, nay*), and terms designating null sets (*nothing, nobody, none*)." Responses that indicated denial include "Like, right here like I can't have the support, I myself, my parents as well but also have my friends as well because they're the ones that's helping, they're supporting me. They're saying, do your homework, you should do this, you go to class, you don't want to fail, you don't want to do this. But, I have to give credit to my parents and also to them. I just not going to say, I'm not going to leave them out because they're the ones as well there helping out as well and they give me support as well"; "Like I said, I don't have really a support system"; and "Yeah, no job, money or nothing like that supports my education, what I wanna do, it just, even without it you can just…" These examples show language of Denial through the phrases "right here, like, I can't have the support" and "Like I said, I don't have really a support system," as each of these statements show that the student did not accept their support system or has chosen not to acknowledge their support system. These results suggest that the students of the net generation may not want support and may reject the support system.

Web-Based Survey

The Web-based survey was used to validate the findings from the previous stages. The role of the web-based survey was to either validate or contradict the participants' responses about the factors that keep students in college. The web-based survey consisted of closed-ended questions, which reflected the manually coded themes that emerged from Diction 6.0, and the responses from the one-on-one interviews.

Participants. This section of the study consisted of 138 participants who attempted to take the online survey. Of these, 16 dropped out of the online survey. To participate in the survey, participants had to meet the following criteria:

1. Age between 18–25
2. Currently enrolled in college
3. Pursuing an Associate degree
4. Have an accumulative 2.0 grade point average (GPA) and
5. Completed at least 12.0 units or four college courses.

If participants did not meet the criteria, they were exited from the survey. For this study, 42 participants did not fit criteria. Responses from the remaining participants were provided using the option of a 5-point Likert scale: (a) strongly agree, (b) agree, (c) neutral, (d) disagree, and (e) strongly disagree.

Demographics. Prior to entering into the online survey, eight demographic questions were presented to the participants. The first demographic question was: "To which racial/ethnic group(s) do you most identify?" Participants' responses were matched to federal mandates of options when asking participants about race in a survey, therefore the options were: (a) White, (b) Black or African, (c) Hispanic or Latino, (d) Asian, (e) Native American and Alaskan Native, (f) Native Hawaiian and Pacific Islander, (g) Two or more races, or (h) Other.

The second demographic question asked the participants to identify their gender. The question provided the option of (a) male or (b) female. Another demographic question asked participants about attendance. Response options for this question were college status: (a) part-time or (b) full-time. A further demographic question inquired about the family background of respondents. Students were requested to choose from a scroll-down option of all the states within the United States and various countries around the world. This was written as: "Choose the state that best describes where your family resides (outside USA will be a choice of country)." Another demographic question inquired about where the students resided. The question was: "Do you live at home with a parent?" The options for response were (a) yes and (b) no.

Students were asked a demographic question that was related to employment: "Which best describes your current employment situation?" The options for response were (a) employed full-time, (b) employed part-time, or (c) unemployed. A furthering demographic question aimed to understand student's financial situation while in college. The question was presented as "Receiving Financial Aid?"

with the options of (a) yes and (b) no. The final demographic question asked about the religious beliefs of the net generation. The respondents were asked to state their religious preference (if any). Responses were according to the options of: (a) Protestant/Christian; (b) Catholic; (c) LDS/Mormon; (d) Jewish; (e) Buddhist; (f) Muslim; (g) No preference/No religious affiliation; (h) Other; or (i) Prefer not to say.

Questionnaire Administration. The opening screen of the questionnaire presented the criteria for the study, as outlined above. Each response was required to fit the criteria; if not, the participant was directed to the exiting screen with a "thank you." The following screen provided the inform consent forms. The informed consent form provided a clear explanation of the study, the roles of participants, and an explanation of the approach to confidentiality. The options available for the consent form were a.) Yes or b.) No. If the participant did not give their consent, they were directed to the exiting screen, with a "thank you."

Human Rights and IRB. Participants in the study remained anonymous: there was no requested information that would identify participants, nor was any tracking method used to identify participants. The participants had access to—and were advised to read— the web-based survey consent form, and if they agreed, they were directed to the survey. The gathered data was stored in a password-protected online secure website, and only I had access to this. The informed consent was an agreement with the participants as to their willing involvement in the study. Participants were made aware that at any time during the web-based survey they were able to exit the survey with no consequences.

Results of Web-Based Survey Questions

The quantitative approach was used to validate (or not validate) the qualitative testimony of the net-generation students, as shown in Table 4.2. This approach was used to obtain an understanding of the following factors (themes) that motivate students' to stay in college.

Theme 1. In response to the theme of Quality/Level of Intimacy that was obtained from the one-on-one interviews, the following question was used in the web-based survey: "In a two-year college I socialize with my friends, my classmates, others who are enrolled in my college, my teammates, or professors." Even though each question was asked separately, the students were able to identify their social surroundings. These social surroundings were built on a framework of which students are able to identify themselves, or to build their own identity. The high percentage shows that students socialize with friends in college. These results answer the research question of "How do students develop their identity?"—from a social perspective—as being "from friends."

Theme 2. For the theme of Characteristics of People, partici-pants in the web-based survey were asked to respond to: "My social group has a group identity, diversity, or similar goals." Even though each question was asked separately, the students were able to identify characteristics of their social group. The results answer the research question of "how do students develop their identity?" by identifying that students in a social group in a college have similar goals.

Theme 3. Responding to the theme of Personal Growth and Self-knowledge, the web-based survey included: "In my two-year col-lege I grew as a person and became more independent, or more aware of my responsibilities." The responses from the survey show that 96% of students became more independent in college and 90% of students claimed that having new responsibilities allowed them to mature as a person. These results suggest that college helps students to develop an identity.

Theme 4. Responding to the theme of Personal Growth and Self-knowledge, another question asked respondents in the web-based survey to reflect on: "By attending a two-year college, I grew as a person." The results show that 58% of students found that their personalities did change while in college. Furthermore, students of the net generation identified the areas of personality that had changed while in college. Even though each question was asked separately, the students were able to identify how they grew as a person in college. This helped to explain the research question of that asked why students choose a college.

Theme 5. Responding to the theme of Environmental Influences or External Control of Change and Individual Control or Internal Control of Change, the web-based survey asked respondents: "What influenced your personality change in a two-year period at college?" The most influential change to college students were found to be environmental influences or external influences. This partially explains why the net generation will choose college.

Theme 6. Responding to the theme of Future Plans, the web-based survey asked the students to respond to: "I chose to go to a two-year college because..." The majority of students responded that they knew what they wanted, with and college being a part of what these students wanted.

Theme 7. Responding to the theme of Social Influences, the web-based survey was the same question as above: "I chose a two-year college because..." Respondents chose from a variety of social influences and benefits to help better themselves.

Theme 8. Responding to the theme of Time of Decision, the web-based survey question was: "I chose to go to a two-year college ..." The majority of respondents replied that they decided after high school. College students of the net generation choose college within a relatively narrow period of time.

Theme 9. Responding to the themes of Learning Standards to Gain a Career or Job of Choice and Learning about Self, the web-based survey is asked participants to respond to: "The benefit of a two-year college is..." Results from the survey show 81% of students felt that the benefit of college is accomplishing the goal of obtaining an associate degree, and 86% found the benefit of college to be transferring to a four-year university/college. This helped to provide some of the reason as to why students chose college.

Theme 10. Responding to the theme of Achieving Goals, the web-based survey asked "The benefit of a two-year college is..." The majority chose "accomplishing a variety of desired goals." This helped to provide some of the reason as to why students choose college.

Theme 11. Responding to the theme of Most Influential, the web-based survey asked participants to respond to: "the greatest influence for me to go to a two-year college is..." This was useful for answering the research question of why college students of the net generation chose college.

Theme 12. Responding to the theme of Comfortable Lifestyle, the web-based survey asked respondents to identify "The most significant impact that influenced my decision to go to a two-year college." The research that asked why the students chose to attend college reflects influences on the students lifestyle. Additionally, the results show that students know and understand what they want their lifestyle to be.

Theme 13. Responding to the theme of Achieving Goals, the web-based survey asked for responses to: "Obtaining a degree or transferring to a university/college is the reason I plan to stay in school next year." The responses to the survey showed that 87% students had chosen to stay in college for the next year to obtain a degree or transfer to a university/college. These results indicate the level of success of students in college.

Theme 14. Responding to the theme of Social Support, Financial Support, and Self Support, the web-based survey asked participants to respond to: "My support system includes..." College students of the net generation outlined that their support system will impact their success in college, and students identified is a variety of support systems.

Theme 15. Responding to the theme of Type of Support and Need for Support, the web-based survey asked participants: "My support system supports me through…" The highest percentage (95%) of responses was for "encouragement." The results for the variety of different types of support helped to identify how successful students were in college. In addition, college students were found to be able to describe their support system effectively in this question.

Theme 16. Responding to the theme of Type of Support and Need for Support, the web-based survey asked respondents to identify "In order to be successful, what I need." The highest percentage was academic support 82%. This identified the answer to the research question of what students need to be successful.

Table 4.2.   Questions, Themes, and Web Results: Correlation

Open-ended Questions	Themes from Interviews	Web Results
1. Whom do you socialize with in college?	Quality/Level of Intimacy	agree: 72% disagree: 28%
	Characteristics of people	agree: 58% disagree: 42%
2. Has your personality changed in college? (How?)	Personal Growth	agree: 60% disagree: 40%
	Self-Knowledge	agree: 82% disagree: 19%
3. What influenced you to change your personality in college?	Environmental Influences or External Control of Change	agree: 73% disagree: 27%
	Individual Control or Internal Control of Change	agree: 66% disagree: 34%
4. When did you decide to go to college?	Future Plans	I know what I want: 56% I want to figure out what I want: 35% What I wanted changed: 6% I do not know: 3%
	Social Influences	agree: 65% disagree: 35%

Open-ended Questions	Themes from Interviews	Web Results
	Time of Decision	Before high school: 10% In high school: 22% After high school: 68%
5. What is the benefit of staying in college? (Short & long term benefits)	Learning standards to gain carrier or job of choice	agree: 71% disagree: 29%
	Learning about self	agree: 86% disagree: 14%
	Achieving Goal	agree: 79% disagree: 21%
6. Do you have a support system to stay in college?	Social Support	agree: 70% disagree: 30%
	Self-Supportive	agree: 66% disagree: 34%
7. Are you planning to stay in school next year? (Why?)	Achieve Goals	agree: 56% disagree: 45%
8. Who influenced you the most to go to college? (How?)	Most influential	agree: 68% disagree: 32%
	Comfortable Lifestyle	agree: 52% disagree: 48%
9. What is your support system that is helping you succeed in college? (How?)	Type of Support	agree: 95% disagree: 5%
	Need for Support	agree: 55% disagree: 45%

CORRELATION OF QUESTIONS, THEMES, AND WEB RESULTS

The relationship between each part of the study was developed following the web-based survey. The data from the one-on-one interviews, transcription, Diction 6.0, and web-based survey were developed to triangulate the data: to better understand the factors that influence students of the net generation to stay in college. The research questions were derived from the same basis: that they would provide a better understanding of students in the net generation and answer the questions of why these students remain in college. The one-on-one interviews were created to gain insight on the students' stories for staying in college, and the findings were further validated with the development of the web-based survey. After the responses from the one-on-one interviews were transcribed and placed into a content text analysis program (Diction 6.0) specific themes emerged, and these were the basis for the close-ended web-based survey. The web-based survey also used eight demographic questions, although the primary reason for the survey was to provide answers for the research questions. A 5-point Likert scale was used for the closed ended questions in the survey to provide statistical data that could validate (or not validate) the data from the one-on-one interviews. The research questions, the one-on-one interview questions and themes, and the themes from Diction 6.0 and the results from the web-based survey.

Correlations

"Who do you socialize with in college?" The respondents during the interview gave their responses about who they identified with socially in college. The results from the interview were the manually coded data. Themes developed from the manually coded data to develop the web-based survey. Data from the manually coding and the survey can be seen to have correlations. Manually coded data showed 8% student-teacher relationships, 10% being socially diverse, 23% social circle, 29% Intimate relationships, and 30% Quality of relationships. Web-based survey showed, 16% socialize with professors, 15% socialize with teammates, 26% socialize with friends, 23% socialize with classmates, and 20% socialize with others enrolled in my college.

"When did you decide to go to college?" The respondents during the interview gave their responses about when they chose and decided to go to college. The results from the interview are the manually coded data. Themes developed from the manually coded data to develop the web-based survey. Data from the manually coded data and the survey have correlations. Manually coded data showed 56% decided to go to college after high school, 16% decided while growing up, and 28% decided in high school. Web-based survey showed 68% decided to go to college after high school, 10% before, and 22% in high school.

"Are you planning to stay in school next year?" The respondents during the interview gave their responses reflected their success in college and explain the reasoning to return the following year. The results from the interview are the manually coded data. Themes developed from the manually coded data to develop the web-based survey. Data from the manually coded data and the survey have correlations. Manually coded data showed 44% goal achievement, transferring, or obtaining degree, and 56% are staying because they want to achieve goals. Web-based survey showed 100% of students plan to stay in school next year is to obtain degree or transfer to a university/college.

Chapter Five

Summary, Conclusions, and Recommendations

SUMMARY

This study aimed to give insight into the college students of the net generation and to develop and understanding of what motivates students to remain in college. Utilizing a phenomenological inquiry, this study allowed net-generation students to tell their story and offered insight into why they remained in college. The mixed-method approach gave a further understanding of the qualitative inquiry, while implementing a quantitative inquiry helped to validate the findings of the phenomenological inquiry. Thus, the sequential method (the two-part study) gives a personal insight (qualitative) and a validation (quantitative) to give further understanding of the reasons why students in the net generation stay in college.

This chapter provides a summary of Chapters 1–4 of to provide insight into the motivations of students of the net generation to remain in college. This summary includes the findings, data collection, and analysis. Additionally, the summary includes discussion, an examination of the research, and an analysis of the research. Based on this, recommendations from the data collection are provided. This summary may give important insights into the net-generation college student and the factors that cause them to stay in school.

Chapter 1 described the issue of retention and college student persistence. Student retention has been an ongoing issue for the past century, and the graduation rates continue to remain at approximately 50% (Swail, 2004). In this context, community colleges serve as a second-chance institution, and the current largest student population in the United States is from the net generation (Tapscott, 2009). Understanding what motivates this generation of students to stay in school is therefore important for improving the current circumstance. Anderson (2003) explained that: "The best predictor of student persistence in college is the student's own motivation/desire to persist" (p. 1). This is the story that needs to be told: it is used to understand the student as an individual and ask the student about their experience of being in college. Chapter 1 identified that the importance of this study lies in its ability to tell the story of net-generation students and explains why they persist through college: this will empower educational institutions to retain students until they are able to graduate.

Chapter 2 presented a review of the literature and delved into the different educational theories that have sought to explain the psychosocial dynamic of the student while in college. Deeply rooted in psychology and focusing on the student, Chickering's identity development was identified as an important psychosocial theory that intended to explain a particular development with tasks or stages in life with humans (Chickering & Reisser, 1993). McClellan et al. (2009) explained that Chickering and Reisser's seven vectors theory would address how students grow and learn in college. William Glasser's (2009) choice theory explained that the reason why students chose college education was related to the fact that it was not mandatory after high school. Edwards (2009) suggested that people have some control of their behavior and thinking, but have limited ability to choose and regulate their emotions and behavior (2009). Choice theory gives insight to a student's initial decision to go to college and the decision to stay despite the various obstacles they encounter. While in college, performance is importance, as students are unlikely to stay in college if they are not performing well. Albert Bandera's (1997) self-efficacy theory explored the reasons why college students have persisted with completing their education.

Chapter 3 identified the research methodology and outlined how the researcher gathered the data. Using a mixed-methods approach, the study was divided into two parts. Part 1 was qualitative and comprised of one-on-one interviews. Part 2 was the quantitative, and used a web-based survey. An additional aspect of the process was the use of the text analysis program Diction 6.0. The responses from the interviews in Part 1 were transcribed, and this data was manually encoded. The transcription was entered into Diction 6.0. Manually encoding the data and the content from Diction 6.0 assisted with creating themes for the study, the themes became a part of the web-based survey, which is part 2 of the study. The web-based survey used to either validate or not validate part 1 of the study and to triangulate the data.

Chapter 4 presented some results from the research. This included data from both parts of the study (the one-on-one interview and part two the web-based survey). Chapter 4 added greater clarity to the correlation of the questions and data collected.

FINDINGS OF THE RESEARCH

The review and analysis of the data included the developed themes, the data from the web-based survey, and an analysis of the research questions. The students of the net generation each have a story to tell that of their journey and experience of being in college. Through these stories, the factors that motivated students to return to college could be effectively identified. The themes revealed in the study give new understanding about the students, and show that students may begin the journey, but do not always finish.

The motivation for students of the net generation to stay in college was high in terms of Cognition and Motion, and low in terms of Familiarity. Question 1 shows low Familiarity when applied to who students socialize: thus, there is a lack of commonality when students are communicating. Cognition and Motion were high in relation to personality change in college. This showed that students learn about their personality and change this in college, although the speed in which this change occurs varies. Question 3 showed high Cognition and low Familiarity. This indicates that students learn about their influences in college, although no a commonality with this exists in relation to the influences for a change in personality.

Questions 4–6 and 8 were high in Cognition and Motion, although low in Familiarity. The results for Question 4 showed that the students were learning about when they made the decision to go to college (although there was no commonality as to when the decision was made), but that the speed it took for the student to make this decision varied. Question 5 was high in Cognition and Motion, although low in Familiarity insofar as this pertains to the benefits of staying in college for either short or long term. Question 6 inquired about student support systems in college, and Question 8 identified who influenced the students the most to go to college. The responses to these questions revealed that the students were still learning (although they do not show a commonality) and the speed for reaching this understanding varied.

Questions 7 and 9 showed high Cognition and low Familiarity. Questions 7 asked students if they planned to stay in college next year, and Question 9 inquired about the support system that helped them succeed. In both questions, students were learning about staying next year or learning about their support system that is helping them succeed in college. However, students were not familiar with each other and thus did not have a commonality to provide a reason for staying over the next year, or the support system helping students succeed in college. In these accounts, each student and each story is different and unique.

CONCLUSION

Analysis of the data and the development of the themes have explained the motivation of the net-generation students and identified the reasons that these students choose to persist through college. Student in college are on a journey and have a story to tell. The student's desires, goals, and aspirations in life mean that they are willing to accept a second chance to achieve what it desired. The information provided below explains the story of the students who chose to stay and persist through college. The themes identify the necessary various factors that will keep a student in college; students who do not possess the various factors that allow them to stay, will not stay.

Research Question 1

In reference to research question 1, "How do students develop their identity in college?" the responses told a story that provided insights for the development of themes. Themes 1–5 explained who students chose to socialize with in college, and Themes 6–8 outlined the characteristics of the people they socialized with in college. Students develop their identity in college by learning about themselves (Theme 9). This leads to their growth as an individual (Themes 10–14). Once students learn their environmental influences or external control of change (Themes 15–18) and their individual control or internal control of change (Theme 19), then, they were able to develop their identity in college.

Research Question 2

In reference to research question 2, "Why did students choose college?" this study found that college is not mandatory, which explains why students would choose to go back to school even though it is not necessary. Theme 20 showed the future-plans of the students in college, wherein some students knew what they wanted, while other students were trying to figure this out. This shows dual reasons as to why students stay in college: they remain in college to either obtain what they want or to figure out what they want. Themes 21 and 23–28 showed that social influences and time of decision (Theme 22) are the reasons that the net-generation students chose college. Themes 29–33 explained the benefits that students gain with education: these benefits influence the desire of students to learn the standards in order to gains the career or job of their choosing. In doing so, students chose to learn about themselves to understand what career or job they want, and students come to understand that attending college or transferring to a college/university and obtaining a degree will increase their chances of gaining the career or job of choice. Students choose college because of their social support (Themes 34–37) and self-support (Theme 38), as all students need a support system to stay in college. Once a student of the net generation chooses to go to college, a support system needs to be incorporated into their educational experience for them to stay. Those involved with support system need to understand that students can be influenced to stay in college (Themes 39–43), and the support systems will have significant influence in this area (Themes 40-47).

Research Question 3

Research Question 3, "How successful are students in college?" led to the following themes. Students were persistent in college by achieving their goals (Theme 48). Themes 49–52 explained the type of support that students need, and identified that students understand and can explain what they need from their support system. This support system was found to be necessary for a student to be successful in college (Themes 53–57). Furthermore, these results showed that students know what they need to be successful in college.

IMPLICATIONS FOR PRACTICE

This study provides insight for educational institutions; or, more specifically, community colleges, as it has examined the motivations of net-generation student to stay in college. The net-generation student's journey through college can be rigorous. However, the student experiences that were recounted for this study have shown that regardless of the difficulty of the journey, students will usually continue their education. Understanding the students' story gives important insight to the motivational process when students choose to stay.

The students of the net generation may or may not understand what it takes to motivate them to stay in college. Not all students have been equipped with the understanding or skill set that will allow them to stay in college. The students who do stay in college have learned about themselves and learned how they have to grow and mature to be successful in the college environment. Additionally, students who stay have learned that they do not have to go through the process of identity development by themselves and that having a support system makes the journey more appealing. Student's past-experiences will provide a foundation for their studies, and will therefore determine the preparedness of the student's ability to persist through college. It is important for educators to understand that when students are integrated or matriculate into college, an effective foundation will allow the student to learn quickly enough to motivate them to stay.

When students of the net generation understand each other, this will result in a stronger relationship developing between students. For the students of the net generation, having positive relationships is essential to their motivation and persistence to stay in college. These relationships will occur at different levels: with friends, with faculty, administrators, and with students attending the school. Some relationships will become intimate, and other relationships will remain work-related. If students are not socializing well or are socially isolated they will not be motivated to stay in college. To address this, an administrator could have a meeting with a student to greet them or inquire about their experiences in the classroom and life outside of the college campus or faculty in the classroom could inquire about a student's day, or take time out of class to allow students to be social with each other. Furthermore, events could be hosted on-campus to allow students to socialize and to establish relationships. The resulting socialization and establishing of relationships could motivate students to persist through college.

Another suggestion is to support students until they are success-ful, as this will increase self-efficacy. The method in which infor-mation is delivered to students should ensure that they understand, as understanding will lead to success. Students of the net generation are often intelligent and well informed because of their continuous access to information on the internet, however, although students have a base knowledge they may not perform well in the classroom. The reason why educational institutions create rigorous standards, curriculums, or assignments needs to be explained to the net-gener-ation students so that they can be successful. For example, students in English language may not feel confident writing a research paper: educators can emphasize the importance of developing the skill of writing, by explaining that the academic writing format will allow the student to practice in-depth of knowledge, critical think-ing, and acquire proficient research skills. When students acquire this understanding, they will become more successful in college, because they will become intrinsically motivated to acquire the skill. Furthermore, the students' performance in college will improve once they acquire new academic skills, and this will encourage them to persist. Through these strategies, students will understand that education involves more than obtaining a degree: that education can change and improve a person's life. Improving an individual's life will also benefit the wider society, because of the services that individual can provide.

On a personal note, my brother emphasized the importance of education, which is the reason why I became a teacher, and—through this process—a scholar. He explained that without teachers little would be achieved. Additionally, a dear friend in my doctoral program explained the difference between a teacher and an educator: a teacher teaches for the time and an educator teaches for a lifetime. These two profound perceptions opened my mind as a researcher and as a scholar, and continue to influence my teaching, which is reflected in the success and influence that I currently have with educating students in the community college. The reason behind sharing this story is it shows the importance of education. What people are taught has an impact on society; therefore a focus on education is important. Formal education is not just a means to gain a degree or employment for a career: it is much more than that, and this has been shown in the current study.

Given that educational institutions—or, more specifically, community colleges—desire to retain students and motivate them to stay in college, they need to implement a student persistence model. A persistence model such as Tinto's Model of Institutional Departure, for example, would help student to persist through college.

One assumption I held prior to the research was that students do not care about college, and are thus not motivated to continue college. However, in the course of this research a couple of themes emerged that showed that students are motivated to continue college. Some students reported that they did not know what they want in college, and emphasized the importance of academic support. Students are attempting to find who they are in academia, and for this reason, they need to be able to identify with college, and while in college be guided through the educational process. Students come from a variety of academic backgrounds and learning capabilities, therefore it is imperative that all students have the academic support that will help motivate them to continue and stay in college.

IMPLICATIONS FOR RESEARCH

In examining net-generation students in college, this study has found that the majority are motivated to stay in college. Students of the net-generation develop their identity in college, or at least develop more of a sense who they are as a person in college. With this insight into themselves, students have a better understanding of which path they will choose, whether it is through education or within the job market. Students are pursuing through college and graduating, although this study has identified a lack of congruency between students and the college. This identifies an opportunity to further motivate students of the net generation to stay in college.

A suggestion for further research into the motivation of the net generation to stay in college is to conduct a study in both a high school and a university (either public or private), and cross analyze the responses from students. The analysis of student responses will provide an insight into the growth levels or maturity students, and this will show the development of identity. Understanding how a student identifies himself or herself with education will give insight into the choices that a student will make in the future in relation to their persistence with a college education. Incorporating some type of tracking method with students, will allow educators to better understand how students mature throughout the education experience. This will assist with identifying how to support and motivate the students to stay in college if they are not able to identify with college or education.

A tracking method with education could also identify differences between the net generation and their motivation to stay in college in relation to the previous generations of students. Researching the veteran generation, baby boomers, generation x, and then the net generation would give insight an each generations perceptions, values, and beliefs systems, which will show a pattern of change. This change could potentially be regulated or the findings could be used to give better understanding for students while in college. For example, students of the net generation have a unique belief and value system that has emerged in relation to preceding generations, and understanding past generations will therefore give a better understanding of the present generation.

Another suggestion for understanding the net-generation students' motivation to stay in college is to research family background. Specifically, an inquiry into a students' background will tell a story about their upbringing. The student's background will also reveal a story about the student's identity in college and the support that they will receive while in college. Students from backgrounds that are positive and who have successful individuals in their family are likely to receive the support that is necessary to the student to persist through college.

Lastly, this study suggests that culture is a motivation for net-generation college students' motivation to stay in college. Students identify themselves with specific cultures, and if the culture does not identify with college, then the student will not stay; on the other hand, if the student is associated with a culture that appreciates education, then they will be able to identify with education and therefore be able to persist through college. Furthermore, in the latter circumstance students will receive the necessary support from the culture that will allow them to persist.

RECOMMENDATIONS FOR IMPLEMENTATION

The overall purpose of this study was to explore the net-generation students and understand their motivation to stay in college. Students were able to articulate the various means of motivation for them and ultimately explain the reasons why they chose to stay in college. It is imperative for education as an institution to understand the student if education is to be able to continue to keep students in school.

The themes suggested in this study indicate that there is a need for a basic level of support if students are going to stay in college. Colleges have programs that students can participate in, although programs are needed where students can first learn about themselves and develop the support that they need. Each student is different, thus any program that focuses on keeping students in school must be able to identify the needs of that student as an individual before prescribing recommendations and giving assistance. Students in this study have shown that a level of intimacy or a certain quality of relationship needed for effective support. This support can be derived from multiple directions, family, friends, faculty, and the educational institution in order to support students through their journey of academia.

When discussing net-generation students, what is being discussed is the student as an individual and an understanding of the factors that will motivate the student of that generation. The net-generation student is unique and is still relatively unknown. Net-generation students are often in conflict with traditional education system approaches, because the relationships that the net generations have had with their parents have them to become more nontraditional. Various scholars have identified that this generation has a sense of entitlement, which indicates that the change in values, beliefs, and perceptions of the world begin within the home. An understanding of the maturity of the student within the home environment will therefore give a better insight as to whether the student will be able to mature quickly enough to stay in college.

Vincent Tinto's model will help aid students of the net-generation students to remain motivated to stay in college. According to Tinto (cited in Swail, 2004; Wild & Ebbers, 2002) the interaction model of student retention explains that there is reciprocal relationship between the social interaction with the student and their commitment to the institution until completion, and that a relationship with the institution and the student affords the best learning environment and experience to the student. The social interaction between student and institution will determine if the student will stay or not. The recommendation for this model is based on the themes of this study: to assist students, faculty, administrators, and the education institution as a whole to understand what motivates students to allow them to persist and stay in college. To provide assistance with students, educational institutions need to understand the process that students go through before they make the decision to not stay, and/or understand the process of students that decide to stay and persist through college.

The Akili model of college student retention (see Figure 5.1) recommends a theoretical framework that will determine if a student of the net generation will stay in college. This model depicts the theoretical framework of: intrinsic motivation, choices of the college student, and college student persistence of the net-generation student. This is an intersection with Vincent Tinto's model of college student departure, and provides suggestions that will motivate college students. Tinto & Cullen's (1973) model states: "Given individual characteristics, prior experiences, and goal commitment, it is the individual's integration into college environment which most directly relates to continuance in college" (p. 43). This provides a theoretical framework for retaining students that will parallel net-generation college students' motivation to be retained.

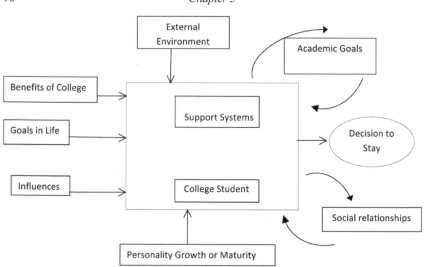

Figure 5.1.   The Akili model of college student persistence

These recommendations are for those who will assist students through their growth process in college. The findings and themes of this study will allow educators to understand what intrinsically motivates students and why they choose college, and to help students persist through college.

The Akili model begins with the student, by examining how the student envisions himself or herself in college, and measures the factors of Personal Growth or Maturity while in college. The interchanging of entities is more prevalent between Academic Goals and Support Systems, the student will achieve academic goals based on the support system and the support system can influence goals. Additionally, Social Relationships and the College Student have an interchanging relationship. The relationships that a student will have in college will depend on the individual student. Moreover, this interaction will affect the relationship between goals of the student and the support system. Influences are the motivational forces that can drive a student to stay (or not stay) in college. This reflects the External Environment, which is outside of the student's control. This includes events that occur in everyday life of the student and that influence the student to stay or not stay. Colleges need to display their point, purpose or benefit to the student that will allow them to stay: thus, the Benefit of College. Everything implied will have an affect a student's Goals in Life. Furthermore, everything implied will affect the support system and college student, therefore influencing the Decision to Stay. Students can experience multiple areas at the same time: for example, Influences and Goals in Life. Viewing the model as cyclical helps to account for where the student is in their development.

This model can be used as a framework assist students with meeting institutional expectations, thus persist through college. The present study has shown that students who are able to meet institutional expectations are likely to persist through college and that educational institutions that able to meet students' needs will encourage students to persist through college. The model is viewed as a continuous flow, with one factor influencing the other: even though it may seem some areas are separate entities, the areas are intrinsically related. For example, Social Relationships reflect Influences, which are continuous, thus reflecting Personality Growth. Support Systems and College student seem to be separate, however they relate to each other because each student is going to require a different type of support. Understanding the student requires and understanding of the support system, and students know what they need, thus these factors are the gatekeepers to understanding what motivates students to stay in college. The surrounding environment impacts the student, and when issues or situations enter their world, this affects their support as well. Additionally, change needs to be considered: a student may have a strong or weak start in education, but this does not mean that their External Environment will not be an Influence for them to leave. Thus, frequent follow-ups are necessary, but contingent upon the student. Therefore, if a student is not responsible and this shows through their social interactions, and no growth is occurring, educational institutions have the power to intervene and help the student. Following the model, it is possible also to consider the reverse: give the student responsibilities, attempt to remove the student from their social environment, or propose a different social environment, and this will allow the student to grow and mature. Additionally, faculty, family, and friends, can help the student grow as a person by being influential figures in the student's life while in college.

The present research tells the story of the student while in college. Educational institutions need to understand the social dynamic and the relationship that the institution has with the students in order to best meet student needs and thereby help them to remain in college. Educational institutions need to understand the uniqueness of the net generation and each student's story before attempting to generalize students. Satisfying the student satisfies the institution, and the process for this is to understand students and the factors that are keeping them in college. This understanding also provides insight into the motivations of those students who are choosing not to stay. This study offers a way to begin to examine this important issue, which is complex and requires an understanding of students in the net generation.

References

Agnes, M. & Guralnik, D. (2002). *Webster's new world college dictionary* (4th ed.). Cleveland, OH: Wiley.

American Association of Community Colleges (AACC). (2012). Directory of member institutions. *American Association of Community Colleges*. Retrieved from http://www.aacc.nche.edu/Pages/CCFinderStateResults.aspx?state=CA

Anderson, E. (2003). *The force field analysis of college student persistence.* Paper presented at the National Conference on Student Retention, San Diego, CA. Retrieved from http://www.apu.edu/strengthsacademy/pdfs/force_field _analysis.pdf

Argosy University. (2010). Internal review board (IRB) handbook.

Bandura, A. (1997). *Self-efficacy: The exercise of control.* New York, NY: W.H. Freeman and Company.

Blance, B. (2004). I taught them but did they learn...?. *International Journal of Reality Therapy, 24*(1), 19–20.

Brophy, J. (2010). *Motivating students to learn.* New York, NY: Routledge.

Burgess, T. (2012). City College 2012–2013 catalog: Fall 2012, spring 2013, summer 2013. *San Diego City College.* Retrieved from http://www.eric .ed.gov/PDFS/ED440671.pdf

Carlson, C., Deloitte & Touche Study (n.d). Traditionalists, baby boomers, generation X, generation Y (and generation Z) working together. Retrieved from http://www.un.org/staffdevelopment/pdf/Designing%20Recruitment,%20Se lection%20&%20Talent%20Management%20Model%20tailored%20to%20 meet%20UNJSPF's%20Business%20Development%20Needs.pdf

Chickering, A., & Reisser, L. (1993). *Education and identity* (2nd ed.). San Francisco, CA: Jossey-Bass.

Cohen, A., & Kisker, C. (2010). *The shaping of American higher education: Emergence and growth of the contemporary system* (2nd ed.). San Francisco, CA: Jossey-Bass.

Cohen, D., & Crabtree, B. (2006). Qualitative research guidelines project. Robert Wood Johnson Foundation. Retrieved from http://www.qualres.org/Home-Tria-3692.html

Conversation... with Rensis Likert. (1973). *Organizational Dynamics, 2*(1), 32–49.

Creswell, J. (2007). *Qualitative inquiry and research design* (2nd ed.). Thousand Oaks, CA: Sage.

Creswell, J. W. (2009). *Research design: Qualitative, quantitative, and mixed methods approaches.* Thousand Oaks, CA: Sage.

Dey, E., & Hurtado, S. (2010). College students in changing context. In Altback, P, Berdahl, R. & Gumport, P. *American higher education in the twenty-first century: Social, political, and economic challenges* (2nd ed., pp. 315–339). Baltimore, MD: Johns Hopkins University Press.

Diction: The text analysis program. (2013, copyright). Retrieved from http://www.dictionsoftware.com/

Edwards, O. W. (2009). A choice theory teaching and learning model for working with children of prisoners. *Educational Psychology In Practice, 25*(3), 259–270.

Elam, C., Stratton, T., & Gibson, D. (2007) Welcoming a new generation to college: The millennial students. *Journal of College Admission. 195*(Spring), 20–25.

Elmore, T. (2010). *Generation iY: Our last chance to save their future.* Atlanta, Georgia: Poet Gardener.

Evans, N., Forney, D., Guido, F., Paton, L., & Renn, K. (2010). *Student development in college: Theory, research, and practice* (2nd ed.). San Francisco, CA: Jossey-Bass.

Glasser, W. (1998). *Choice theory in the classroom* (Rev. ed.). New York, NY: Harper Perennial.

Holland, N. N. (2001). "The barge she sat in": Psychoanalysis and diction. *Psychoanalytic Studies, 3*(1), 79–94.

Howe, N. & Strauss, W. (2000). *Millennials rising: The next great generation.* New York, NY: Vintage Books.

Jensen, U. (2011). *Factors influencing student retention in higher education.* Honolulu, HI: Kamehameha Schools–Research & Evaluation Division, Pacific Policy Research Center. Retrieved from http://www.ksbe.edu/spi/PDFS/Retention_Brief.pdf

Kahlenberg, R. (2010, October 1). The community college summit. *The Chronicle of Higher Education.* Retrieved from http://chronicle.com/blogs/innovations/the-community-college-summit/27361

Kalsner, L. (1991). Issues in college student retention. *Higher Education Extension Review, 3,* 1–6. Retrieved from http://eric.ed.gov/PDFS/ED350894.pdf

Karp, H., Fuller, C., & Sirias, D. (2002). *Bridging the boomer xer gap: Creating authentic teams for high performance at work.* Palo Alto, CA: Davies-Black.

King, J. E. (2003). Nontraditional attendance and persistence: The cost of students' choices. *New Directions For Higher Education, 121,* 69.

Kit-Ling, L. (2009). Grade differences in reading motivation among Hong Kong primary and secondary students. *British Journal of Educational Psychology, 79*(4), 713–733.

Kitzinger, J. (1995). Introducing focus groups. *British Medical Journal, 311*, 299–302. Retrieved from http://www.ncbi.nlm.nih.gov/pmc/articles/PMC2550365/pdf/bmj00603-0031.pdf

Krueger, R., & Casey, M. (2000). *Focus groups: A practical guide for applied research* (3rd ed.). Thousand Oaks, CA: Sage.

Kuh, G. et.al. (2008). Unmasking the effects of student engagement on first-year college grades and persistence. *Journal of Higher Education, 79*(5), 540–563.

Lau, L. (2003). Institutional factors affecting student retention. *Education, 124*(1)*, 126–136*. Retrieved from http://www.uccs.edu/Documents/retention/2003%20Institutional%20Factors%20Affecting%20Student%20Retention.pdf

Leedy, P. D., & Ormrod, J. E. (2005). *Practical research: Planning and design.* Upper Saddle River, NJ: Pearson Prentice Hall.

Leppel, K. (2005). College persistence and student attitudes toward financial success. *College Student Journal, 39*(2), 223–241.

Lowe, S., & Skarl, S. (2009). Talkin' 'bout my generation: Exploring age-related resources. *College & Research Libraries News, 70*(7), 400–403. Retrieved from http://crln.acrl.org/content/70/7/400.full

Lowe, W. (2002). *Software for content analysis—A review*. Cambridge, MA: Weatherhead Center for International Affairs and the Harvard Identity Project. Retrieved from http://www.wcfia.harvard.edu/misc/initiative/identity/

Loyd, B. D. (2005). The effects of reality therapy/choice theory principles on high school students' perception of needs satisfaction and behavioral change. *International Journal of Reality Therapy, 25*(1), 5–9.

Maehr, M., & Meyer, H. (1997). Understanding motivation and schooling: Where we've been, where we are, and where we need to go. *Educational Psychology Review, 9*(4), 371–409. doi: 10.1023/A:1024750807365

Maehr, M., & Midgley, C. (1991). Enhancing student motivation: A schoolwide approach. *Educational Psychologist.* 26(3 & 4), 399–427. Retrieved from http://www.unco.edu/cebs/psychology/kevinpugh/motivation_project/resources/maehr_midgley91.pdf

McClellan, G., Stringer, J., & Associates. (2009). *The handbook of student affairs administration* (3rd ed.). San Francisco, CA: John Wiley & Sons.

Merrow, J. (2007). Community colleges: The (often rocky) path to the American dream. *Change, 39*(6), 14–21.

Mottern, R. (2008). Choice theory as a model of adult development. *International Journal Of Reality Therapy, 27*(2), 35–39

Office of Institutional Research and Planning (2012). Fact book city college. *San Diego City College.* Retrieved from http://research.sdccd.edu/docs/Research%20Reports/College%20and%20District%20Fact%20Books/2012/City_FactBook_2012.pdf

Patton, M. Q. (2002). *Qualitative research and evaluation methods.* Thousand Oaks, CA: Sage.

Phillippe, K., & Patton, M. (2000). National profile of community colleges: Trends and statistics 3D edition. *American Association of Community Colleges.* Retrieved from http://www.eric.ed.gov/PDFS/ED440671.pdf

Price, C. (2010). Why don't my students think I'm groovy?: The new "R"s for engaging millennial learners [*PsychTeacher* listserve]. Retrieved from: http://www.drtomlifvendahl.com/Millennial%20Characturistics.pdf

Pullian, J., & Patten, J. (1999). History of education (7th ed.). Upper Saddle River, NJ: Prentice-Hall.

Pusser, B., & Levin, J. (2009). Re-imagining community colleges in the 21st century: A student-centered approach to higher education. *Center for American Press.* Retrieved from: http://www.americanprogress.org/issues/2009/12/pdf/community_colleges_reimagined.pdf

Rainer, T. & Rainer, J. (2011). *The millennials: Connecting to America's largest generation.* Nashville, TN: B&H Publishing Group.

Strauss, L & Volkwein, J. (2004). Predictors of student commitment at two-year and four-year institutions. *The Journal of Higher Education, 75*(2), 203–227. Retrieved from: http://muse.jhu.edu/login?auth=0&type=summary&url=/journals/journal_of_higher_education/v075/75.2strauss.html

Swail, W. (2004). The art of student retention: A handbook for practitioners and administrators. *Educational Policy Institute.* Retrieved from http://www.educationalpolicy.org/pdf/ART.pdf

Tapscott, D. (2009). *Grown up digital: How the net generation is changing your world.* New York, NY: McGraw-Hill.

Troxel, W. (2010). Student persistence and success in United States higher education: A synthesis of the literature. *EvidenceNet.* Retrieved from http://www.heacademy.ac.uk/assets/EvidenceNet/Syntheses/US_retention_synthesis.pdf

Wild, L., & Ebbers, L. (2002). Rethinking student retention in community colleges. *Community College Journal of Research and Practice, 26,* 503–519.

Williams, J. (2010). Understanding first-year persistence at a micropolitan university: Do geographic characteristics of students' home city matter? *College Student Journal, 44*(2), 362–376.

Wlodkowski, R. (2008). *Enhancing adult motivation to learn: A comprehensive guide for teaching all adults* (3rd ed.). San Francisco, CA: Jossey-Bass.